The
ROYAL ARCH
JOURNEY

Rev Neville Barker Cryer

Lewis Masonic

First published 2009
Reprinted 2020

ISBN 978 0 85318 331 0

Published by Lewis Masonic

an imprint of Ian Allan Publishing Ltd, Shepperton, Middx TW17 8AS.
Printed in England.

Visit the Lewis Masonic website at www.lewismasonic.co.uk

This book is dedicated to HARRY MENDOZA.
A conscientious Mason, keen Companion and fellow Q.C. researcher
with immense thanks and respect.

Contents

Introduction

Anyone daring to write yet another book on the subject of the Royal Arch needs to be very clear about its purpose. Does it add anything to what has been published previously on the subject, bearing in mind that all earlier works are now either out of print or probably tucked away in some rarely used Masonic Hall library?

This book is certainly produced with two main objectives in mind. One is to try and tell the story of how the degree, only later known as the Order of the Holy Royal Arch, emerged in England and then developed up to 1835, but without undue diversions on the way. The other aim is to show, through that story, why the Holy Royal Arch of Jerusalem is an essential step for a truly Free and Accepted Mason and has for so long been regarded as the culmination, as the *summum bonum,* of English Freemasonry.

These have been the clear objectives.

Declaring these two objectives, of course, means that certain restrictions are placed on my story. Those who want to discover the details of any personalities mentioned, to study all the changes in its regalia or tracing boards, the subtler meanings of the ritual, the minutiae of varied or foreign Constitutions and the statistics of membership or the order of precedence of individual Chapters, will not find help here. For most of these subjects the comprehensive work of Bernard E. Jones in *The Freemasons Book of the Royal Arch* (1969) is still available and contains much that needs no repetition. More recent publications by Companions Wells, Sandbach, Mendoza, or even my own recent work, *What Do You Know about the Royal Arch?* will provide information for any researching in other fields.

My purpose here is narrower and sharper, as well as having a shorter time-scale.

However, whilst it may be much more limited this does not mean that it has been much simpler to complete. It would be foolish to embark on this story without having first become acquainted with the paths previously taken.

Many notable Masonic scholars and writers have ventured upon a similar journey or some part of it and not to have considered their findings and arguments would be both foolish and ungenerous. There will, I hope, be ample recognition in what follows of the debt owed to those whose work is now either out of print or, more probably, out of mind.

It is obviously impossible, as it is unnecessary, to name all those whose former efforts and study have made what follows possible, but the works of Gould, Carr, Castells, Clarke, Eric Ward, Bernard Jones and Batham need especial mention because they pioneered ways that can now be described and assessed. Some would contend that even the work of the Revd Dr George Oliver ought not to be wholly overlooked even if it is treated with some caution.

There are, of course, those who assert, as with the beginnings of Free and

Accepted Craft Freemasonry, that our Royal Arch origins are so shrouded in mystery as unlikely ever to be disclosed.

I do not share that opinion.

My own pondering on, and engaging with, the material made available in the last century and a half, confirms me in the view that there is an adequate thread running through our present knowledge of the past to allow an acceptable, understandable and reliable story to be told.

Certainly, there may still be parts of this journey about which a final conclusion cannot yet be claimed. Where that is so, I hope that I have set out the case for alternative explanations or made clear a problem that still needs a more satisfactory solution. That, I believe, could also be a further goal for the future; that we should disclose what later researchers will have yet to clarify or discover.

In starting to reconstruct the earlier story of the Royal Arch there is one stumbling block that has to be overcome at once. This is the persistent, and quite understandable contention that what we are looking for as a starting point is some form or name of the Order which is familiar to us today. The Holy Royal Arch as we know it did not suddenly spring into view, so that all we have to do is to discover when and where this event took place. That is what many have sought.

Would that it were so easy. It is not.

Indeed, it is just because it is not that easy that the idea of its start being totally shrouded in mystery persists. And what is true of the form of this degree is also true of the name. I will seek to show that the kernel of the Royal Arch was present before ever it was known by this particular title.

What we are in danger of doing is looking for the wrong thing in the wrong place.

We can so easily think that we know exactly what it is we are looking for or what it is that we expect to discover and where that would be most likely to appear. When this does not happen we either claim that the Royal Arch origins are unknowable or that they are unlikely to be discovered with our present knowledge. As Douglas Knoop so helpfully pointed out:

> 'the claim of the Royal Arch to be part of "Pure Ancient Masonry" can be judged, not by trying to trace the (name) "Royal Arch" back to 1717 or so, but by considering whether the principal esoteric knowledge associated with the Royal Arch can be shown to have existed when the Premier Grand Lodge was founded (1717). If that can be shown to be the case... then the Royal Arch can claim to be part of "Pure Ancient Masonry" with as much justification as the Three Craft Degrees.' (B.E. Jones: Freemasons Book of the Royal Arch, 1969 edn. p.114)

My belief is that there is such a track to be followed even if it may at first seem to be in unlikely territory. What that track is, will I trust, become clear as we proceed on our journey. What first led me to this way of thinking about sources was my recall of the stories about those who went in search of the sources of the Nile and the Amazon, as well as having once enjoyed a description of the course of the River Tees. In the former two cases the search was frequently in danger of being wholly abandoned because the clues pointing to their sources were confusing and sometimes quite misleading. The discovery of TWO Niles was itself a huge surprise. In the case of the Tees the author had eventually to recognise that its real source was so imperceptible as to be easily overlooked.

The similarities between these experiences and our present Holy Royal Arch enquiry are not entirely perfect but they are close enough to caution the reader against any tendency to hasty judgment or easy dismissal.

What I am saying is that unless we are prepared to consider evidence that may seem unlikely, as well as the many other leads that have from time to time been perhaps insufficiently examined, we are unlikely to reach a satisfactory goal.

There are, however, more things to be said.

The first concerns an insight that was expressed clearly in a paper presented by Bro Michael Baigent to Quatuor Coronati Lodge. Pursuing the involvement of those who were also Freemasons in the activities of the Royal Society from its inception, he was eager to distinguish between two aspects of our own Society. One was the ORGANISATION and structure of Freemasonry, its function in and through Lodges or Chapters, its forms of government and ceremonial, and what might be called *'its working skeleton'*. Study of how that skeleton had developed and adapted as time and customs altered is important, but we have to beware of thinking that that is the only aspect that defines our organisation.

What is just as important, and some even go on to claim as superior, is what must be called the CONTENT of traditional instruction, the tenets and principles, the allegorical and legendary elements that are contained within the historical structure.

What Bro Baigent was suggesting was that, as we come to study either Free and Accepted Masonry in itself or, as is now much more frequently the case, its relationship with the people of this and other lands, we need to define more carefully than hitherto which aspect of our society is being dealt with. It has been the cause of too much misunderstanding simply to use the terms *Freemasonry* or *Freemasons* without much more precise definition.

You surely know what I mean.

When writers tell us that Rosicrucians, Kabbalists, coffee houses or even Francis Bacon were the formative influences on Freemasonry, I am bound to ask: *'how have they been formative and of what?'* Are we talking about their influence on our organisation and structure, or on what we do or what we have professed? The answers we then get are the significant ones.

Talking about being more clear and precise as to what exactly we are discussing or examining, I decided some time ago to mark my argument by the printing type to be employed. For all stonemasonry activity of the operative kind I have used the lower case. Hence, mason, warden, lodge or guild, when speaking of operatives, while I use capital initials for Masonic Work in its Accepted phase, which of course persists to the present time. This at least helps us to know, as author and reader, who or what is the more precise subject of our study.

I have to say that I have spent far too much time in the past wondering exactly what kind of mason/Mason or lodge/Lodge I was supposed to be focusing on. I can, for instance, fully concur in the idea of masons in ancient Babylon or Egypt and freestone masons in medieval times but Freemasons are only relevant in another and much later era.

To assist the reader in some way with this distinction, will be evident in all that I write from now on.

There remain just two more matters needing comment.

It soon becomes evident to any student of the last 200 years that what has been taking place, slowly but surely, is a constant diminution in the content of what Freemasonry has sought to express and to teach.

Nowhere is this as evident as in the study which is presented here. Moreover, it is not just the curtailing or dispensing of certain ceremonial aspects but the right to acquire the knowledge of those and the still remaining knowledge that is affected. What was once regarded as essential revelation worth striving for, has now become so much less easily available. The facts will reveal their own picture and perhaps explain why some (or is it many?) Masons declare that the Holy Royal Arch is hard to understand.

Lastly, work on this book was begun before the changes made in the conduct of the Holy Royal Arch in late 2004. Some of the evidence that is provided here, and the conclusions thus reached about earlier understandings of our Order, may seem to run counter to what has been authorised recently by the Supreme Grand Chapter of England. Let me hasten to say that in setting out this narrative no disrespect for, or demur from, the present regulations has been or is intended. As a Masonic historian I am concerned simply with what we can properly affirm about our Order's early practice and growth. If those in the Order today now wish to guide the Order's future along a different path, that is their right and privilege. What was done at the outset of the Holy Royal Arch's existence 300 or even more years ago can be properly deemed by some to have no relevance to our contemporary scene.

I must state clearly that what will be set out here was never intended to suggest any other implication. Just to have the early history retold as faithfully and straightforwardly as the facts allow, even if from some new angles, is and has been my sole desire.

All that said, and with every confidence that this tale will be one to interest and encourage both Holy Royal Arch Companions or even other Brethren in this new millennium, who might, as a result of reading this story, be attracted to join our Order, let us set out on our journey.

Back to our Sources

To anyone familiar with the subject of Royal Arch sources it soon becomes clear that there have been a number of theories as to how this form of Freemasonry began.

In 1991, Bro Anthony Ough presented his Batham Lecture entitled 'The Origin and Development of Royal Arch Masonry: A Short History of the Evolution of the Organisation and the Ritual'.

In the course of that lecture he very usefully described four most likely sources which had been subject to some detailed examination by others. He described them as follows:

(a) '...that it was a Ceremony existing in Ireland from ancient times'. He adds, however, that it is not named in those important Irish documents, Pennell's Constitutions of 1730 nor in Spratt's Constitutions of 1744.
(b) '...that it was an importation from the Continent'. There was, he goes on to say, a Jacobite supporters's complex system of Masonry expounded by the Chevalier Ramsay, and though it appears that he did have a meeting with Bro. Laurence Dermott of the Antients there was apparently no collaboration.
(c) '...that it was a fabrication by Laurence Dermott and others, designed as a justification for the creation of the Antients Grand Lodge by laying claim to a greater measure of antiquity and of possession of secrets not known to the Premier Grand Lodge'.
(d) '...that in the process of development of ritual it was a mutilation of the third degree to form a fourth. However, such chronological evidence as is available is inconclusive'.

Bro Ough therefore concluded that *'there are a number of theories but only a collection of singular facts which are insufficient to constitute any conclusive evidence of the origin of Royal Arch Masonry... This being the case its early development may have been for the purposes already stated in (c) but it is still a matter of conjecture. The consensus of Masonic opinion is that the facts may never become known.'* (AQC Vol. 108. p.189)

This is a useful, more contemporary, summary of what were considered the most dependable 'origin' theories, and not what he calls, but does not describe as, the fanciful ones.

It is interesting to note the doubts he expresses as to why he considers even these answers to be problematical. However, in my opinion his approach, like most others on the subject, still suffers from overlooking two factors. One of these is that this journey properly needs to begin at a time significantly earlier than that which is normally considered. It has to be asked whether the events of 1550-1717 do not have an essential bearing on our study.

That is a huge question if you still believe, as I was once brought up to believe, that our English Freemasonry does not really begin until the founding of the Premier Grand Lodge. That, let me here affirm, I most certainly do not any longer believe. Our Free and Accepted roots are much deeper.

This was made plain in an address given by Bro Heron Lepper, PSGD and Past Grand Superintendent of the Tabernacle in Ireland, when he spoke to the Supreme Grand Chapter of England, in November 1933:

'I hold that the Degree of Royal Arch is as English in its origin as any of the Craft degrees and that in its essentials it is part and parcel of the tradition handed down to us by our predecessors of the pre-Grand Lodge era.'
(Quatuor Coronati copy 19328)

I shall have occasion to use more of his observations later.

The other factor that I believe Bro Ough overlooks, and of course he is far from being alone in this, is what was briefly referred to in the Introduction. It is that we must not consider ourselves limited in this search to just those occasions when there is some mention of the terms 'Arch' or 'Royal Arch'.

I believe that we have to take seriously some features in the Old Charges and earliest ritual remnants that give us clues as to what was already known and shared. To be precise, I believe that our Royal Arch journey really begins with the 'structures' and the 'content' first familiar to our operative guild forebears.

Here, the reader must understand that there is a difference between what took place in a Guild court and Lodge, as compared with an assembly and lodge on a working site of stonemasons. We shall shortly turn our attention to examining these two factors as they lead us up to the events of the early 18th century.

What such an examination will, in fact, be doing is clarifying that earlier tradition of which Heron Lepper makes mention. One of the constant claims of some English Freemasons from the 1730s was that the working of the Premier Grand Lodge had already diverged from the practices of ancient Masonry.

What 'ancient' here meant was not the workings of the Anglo Saxon, Solomonic or Egyptian periods, whatever they may, or may not have been. What was being referred to by this complaint was that the new Grand Lodge was ignoring important elements in what had developed in the preceding 200 years. It is to discover what some of that tradition was that is the purpose of what follows.

The Changing Role of the Master Mason
When working stonemasons were engaged on the impressive building projects that produced such works as the Minster at York, the cathedral at Strasbourg, the walls of Carcassonne in the Languedoc or the citadel of Krak des Chevaliers in Syria, they were organised in a comparatively simple but clearly defined manner.

A master mason – in consultation with the patrons of the works being undertaken, whether a monarch, a group of monks or clergy, or the principal officers of a diocese or borough – conceived and drew up a plan. The plan would cover not only the general outline and design of the structure, but would indicate all major and minor features, the various materials required and types of workmen who would be employed, along with an estimate of their wages. As I have elsewhere shown in a book on the building of York, a master mason had to be a specially educated and experienced person who could undertake the combined tasks of what we would now describe as an architect, surveyor, treasurer and clerk of works.

The training for this important and responsible post required a working knowledge of most, if not all, of the stonemasons' skills, a period of learning on different sites under other master masons, detailed and informed study of the seven Liberal Arts and Sciences, and a proven ability to keep and share those 'mystic secrets' which we are now more familiar with as geometry, trigonometry and calculus. Anyone doubting this level of skill need only consider the work of a master mason like the Greek, Phidias, who designed and oversaw the construction of the Acropolis in Athens.

What has become even clearer as this book was being researched and written is the new awareness among scholars of the education that was provided by the monasteries and cathedral schools from the 11th century onwards.

As Bro De Lafontaine, who was the Prestonian Lecturer for 1930, expressed it:

'The liberal man meant, in the Middle Ages, the man who was his own master. The Master Masons of those days, always anxious to elevate their profession above the position of a mere operative art, readily assumed these liberal arts and sciences as a part of their course of knowledge, thus seeking to assimilate themselves rather to the then scholars who were above them than to the workmen who were below them.' (Collected Prestonian Lectures vol. 1. p.124)

Alongside this proof of the knowledge that was to be acquired by master masons and, I should add, master carpenters is the fact that such men were the only persons amongst the building craftsmen who were permitted to meet with the monks, clergy or Templar knights in their Chapter assemblies, or to sit at the high table of a king or nobleman as their companions.

In the will of Bishop William of Wykeham, the founder of the notable school at Winchester and New College at Oxford, there is specific mention of the Bishop's master of the work on both these projects. The Bishop states that '

Master William Wynford is to be received as a special brother of our Chapter and that there be done for him in life and after death as for one of the brothers of our congregation.'

That was in 1399, showing that a master mason was by then a privileged person. On another side of this social arrangement we find in many forms of medieval regulation that, once appointed to the post of master mason, this 'officer' was no longer part of the working lodge of stone craftsmen. His only contact with that institution was to recommend what apprentices should be trained there; to knock on the door of the lodge, if necessary, when the craftsmen were due to attend labour; and, via the lodge warden, to summon the necessary specialists or foremen from the lodge so as to share with them, in his own tracing room or area, the plans or outlines of that section of the structure which was next to be prepared or erected. He would also be the one to consult with leading members of the lodge about any proposed wage changes. It is quite true that ancient Masonry knew three grades but the differences between them were much more marked than we have acknowledged.

The master mason was an important person. He was paid substantially more than others. He alone wore a hat and robe, carried a wand or rod of office and always wore gloves when on the work site to show that he was not engaged in the tasks of ordinary craftsmen. Amongst the latter no gloves were worn save on cold or wet days when a special piece of masonry had to be manhandled into a particularly difficult position. The master mason was thus distinctive and was the pre-eminent representative of the stone building trade.

In some cases he was called, as we have seen, 'The master of the work' and, with the master carpenter, supervised everyone else on the working site. This is why, in many medieval scenes of masons at labour he is shown alongside the king, bishop or nobleman who is inspecting the work.

Nicholas de Biard in the later 13th century wrote:

'In these great buildings it is the custom to have a chief master who only directs things by word (and) seldom or never lays hand to the work himself...' (Hiscock p. 171)

It is here that the first firm clue to what we are looking for is found, the status of what can only be described as a 'True Master Mason'. One might also remark that the similarities in dress with eventual Royal Arch regalia is noticeable, that is, head-gear, a rod, a robe and gloves. That seems to be saying clearly that this is still what the dress of a true Master Mason should be.

It has therefore to be remembered that throughout the medieval period there was a clear and recognised distinction between this office and that of the fellows or master craftsmen who carried out all the different forms of specialist construction. The understanding of this division of labour is not one that has been generally appreciated by Freemasons with the result that there has been much misunderstanding about the place of 'Masters' and the Lodge.

Having established the distinction between the master mason and the rest of the working stonemasons in terms of how the stonemasons' trade operated we now have to examine the difference that existed between what the master masons knew, as compared with the knowledge that was usual amongst the various kinds of craftsmen.

Whilst they all shared a common acquaintance with the purpose and use of certain tools; e.g. the chisel, the maul, the hand-pick, the lever, the lewis, the chain and pulley, the square and compasses amongst others, the master mason was possessed of seven more essential skills at least. He was trained in the whole content of the Seven Liberal Arts and Sciences and these at once gave him distinctive traits. By Grammar he knew how to read and to write; by Logic he discovered how to tackle a problem and reason a case; by Rhetoric he knew how to share the ideas that he might have with others; by Music he learnt the art of harmony and sound, essential in constructing both halls and churches; by Arithmetic he could calculate quantities and dimensions whilst by Geometry he could calculate the precise details of construction. With Astronomy, or astrology, and both were closely associated until the late 17th century, he had the tools with which to learn the ordered patterns of the heavens, the seasons of the year and the periods most propitious for labour. He was made privy to the mystery of the Zodiac known from Babylonian times.

Yet the greatest skill was his access to the core secret of all ancient and medieval building practice, the way to form a right-angled triangle, then the heart of practical geometry. The 3:4:5 pre-positional nature of this insight was of singular significance in the journey we are making. It was the justification for the claim that at the pinnacle of the stonemason's trade there had to be 'a rule of three'.

This 'rule of three', to which we shall constantly return, was emphasised by the stonemasons' guild banner with its triple motto 'In deo spero' (In God I trust) for the God in whom these first Accepted Masons were to place their trust was a Deity with a threefold personae: Father, Son and Holy Ghost.

This is a principle that links in an unbreakable line the ancient operative trade, the form of that trade in the Guild and the completion of Free and Accepted Masonry as it emerges in the 18th century. It is a theme that confirms the evolution of what was eventually called Royal Arch Masonry – the final component of a process that emerged from the earliest times.

A Master Mason was one who held the ultimate secrets.

Yet it was not just special knowledge that distinguished the working master masons. In his comments on a paper given in Quatuor Coronati Lodge in 1926, Bro Worts made another important contribution to our present subject. He wrote:

'The Masters were the "great ones"; they directed and probably controlled whatever organisation the masons had; they were therefore "oathed" first, not last; they were "bound" in economic and legal obligations to their employers. That was the public side of the business. But there was another side – their own private side; they knew much, "the last and highest things" which made them powerful in the eyes of kings and priests. How best to defend this status and all it meant? A formula of ADMISSION and MEMBERSHIP of this "circle" was devised, a terse but binding "ceremony" was undertaken by any

*new entrant privileged to join; the Holy Church, being at hand and very
interested, soon invested this "ceremony" with the essential religious "taboos";
the "oath" came; so did the "WORD" and the "Name" in the course of time.
The "Name" chosen embodied the ideals of the Master Builder... (&) perhaps
there was an overriding single Name...' (p.39. AQC vol.72) (my emphases)*

The era of the multi-purpose master mason – with the separate offices of designer,
surveyor, works and financial manager – would begin to fade during the late 16th
century. It would persist in the more formal and allegorical setting of the Guild
and Guild Lodge that then took on a new prominence.

It was in this new Guild setting that the earliest arrangement of a master mason
who was set apart, and a working lodge ruled over by a warden, who was elected
by the fellows, was steadily replaced by a Right Worshipful Master assisted by two
Wardens.

You may notice that this is again the 'rule of three'.

The similarity of this arrangement to the then parish church requirement of an
Incumbent and two Wardens was no coincidence. Not surprisingly, those who
now attended the Lodge but had not been working stonemasons, assumed, as do
Freemasons today, that the form of a Lodge they first encounter, *'for its well ruling
and governing'*, is that which had always been the case.

That, of course, is not so.

What we have to be aware of is that one of the main reasons why the first non-
operatives joined the masons' guild or its lodge was because as citizens of the local
town or borough they had been deprived of, and sorely missed, their former
parish, Saints and community guilds and hence some sought to join their closest
remaining alternative.

It is all the more understandable that they would appreciate a form of
organising a Lodge that was nearest to what they had been accustomed to in their
sacred associations.

This old tradition had a marked Christian spirit. Bro Castells, thinking of the
Old Testament content of so much ritual, claims that the background to our Craft
was Jewish. I am sure he was mistaken, unless he meant Judaeo-Christian.

Yet there were other dimensions to the changeover from operative to Guild or
Accepted Freemasonry.

One of these was the continuing presence in this new kind of Lodge of those
who were still professional stonemasons. They, no doubt, were those who helped
to influence the methods of opening and closing a Lodge of Fellows, of examining
and obligating candidates, of maintaining and reciting the Regulations and
recalling the traditions of the 'old masons' in what were called the 'Old Charges',
including their 'colourful' history.

It was the influence of such working Brethren that ensured the continuing of
the practice whereby the Wardens still regulate the opening and closing of a Lodge

and examine the competency of candidates. They were also the means by which the ancient status of the Master Mason was still recognised even though some prosperous master craftsmen were able to apply for membership of the Guild. That such men were both jealous for, and zealous in, their protection of the 'old ways' is revealed in the York scene as late as the mid-18th century.

However, it is now time to pass to the next stage of this particular story.

During the reigns of the Tudor monarchs the English trade of stonemason underwent a severe change. Not only did building in stone decline considerably, being replaced by timber and brick construction, but also stonemasons suffered the grievous pain of seeing so many of the sites that would have usually been a source of labour for extension, repair or maintenance now being demolished or neglected.

Not unexpectedly, there was a change in the economic practice of a master mason.

Even before this period of major change the master mason had begun to diversify his role. He changed from being mainly a designer-architect to becoming an entrepreneur employer of craftsmen and apprentices. He set up business as a purveyor of memorial tablets, tombs and gravestones, and in York, as elsewhere, he assumed a municipal role as inspector of new constructions, whether private houses or public institutions. He also appeared as an influential member of the Masons' Trade Guild or Company. What, we have to ask, is his exact status and function in this new milieu, even if, as in the case of York, a guild had been known to exist from the mid-14th century at least?

The next distinction is that it was already the custom in large towns for the wealthiest members of the trade companies to be required to accept the honour, and discharge the duties, of Mayor and Aldermen as well as of other offices. It is hardly surprising that the combination of wealth and influence now often led to those who had been master masons and were now successful business men, being preferred as Masters of their companies and so local town or city officers.

Moreover, by the 17th century several Masons' Guilds had a Lodge attached and, as some Old York Charges reveal, any Freeman of the city could apply for Lodge membership if he was willing to submit to the Guild requirements in so far as they applied to him. This development would be reinforced by the custom in the Guild or Company of adopting the Old Charges as the basis for regulating new admissions.

Thus we note that when the new candidate was required to swear allegiance to the Company's or Lodge's rules it is 'The ANCIENTS', the SENIORS, who present the book and administer the oath.

I have just discovered that, in Coventry, the 'Ancients' were the senior RULERS in the craft.

Already we can clearly discern the continuance of a superior grade of member whose status is expressed in ceremonial practice.

By the 1660s it became normal for this kind of Master to be elected by the past rulers of the Company, for him to be senior in membership and someone of social standing as well as of some affluence. Those in Livery Companies to this day will know that progress to the Chair of a Company is not by rote but by careful selection by the Past Masters. It would hardly be unusual if, in a Masons' Guild, aspirants for such a post were more likely to be those who had previously been, or were descendants of, master masons.

A natural transition from a working master mason to Guild Master had begun to take place.

As I have explained elsewhere in my book *Did You Know This Too?*, the new need and desire of working stonemasons in the 1670s period, for a fresh charter and guild, representing a marked improvement in their trade meant that the Lodges that had been attached to the old guild were now left on their own as private Lodges.

So these Lodges had to discover a new basis of authority for their existence as the old guild oversight ceased to function. In this situation the old mantle and title of Master Mason was resumed. A Master Mason was one who had occupied the chair of an Accepted Masons Lodge and who had been made privy to the secrets and privileges of that position. Whether there were any 'particular secrets' we shall consider before I end this chapter but that there was a grade of Master Mason when the 18th century begins is proved for me by at least two facts.

The first fact is that in London by 1716 four private Lodges such as we have seen emerging were seeking a new authority for, and over, themselves. What they sought was a different kind of Grand Lodge from that which had formerly ruled the building guilds of London and Westminster. When the form of that Grand Lodge had been agreed, the Lodge members needed to appoint a Grand Master.

Whom did they choose?

We may be surprised that they selected a tradesman/bookseller, Bro Anthony Sayer. What is significant and interesting is that he is described as being the one suitable because he was *'the senior Master Mason among them'*.

This tells us three things:

1. That it was by now quite normal for a person who was not a working stonemason to be one of the rulers in their Accepted Craft.
2. That there was a recognised status and role for a Master Mason in these Lodges and that role in no sense related to a trade qualification. He was a ceremonial Master Mason.
3. That there were in these Lodges other Master Masons and even a sense of seniority among them, so that, as *'the most senior'*, which surely had to mean by service and not by age, Sayer was fit to be suggested for, and supported in, the post of Grand Master. Master Masons, as rulers, are, from its start, part and parcel of the new Premier Grand Lodge make-up. In at least two contemporary ritual sources, Master Masons are seen as 'rulers of their Lodge'.

That is not the whole story, however. I said that there were two facts that supported the view that Master Masons are part of early Accepted Masonry. The second evidence comes from York and is the fact that among the records at Duncombe Place in that city there is a list of 15 men who are registered Master Masons in the Grand Lodge of All England at York in the period before 1724.

This list not only registers certain Freemasons before 1717 but indicates that a grade of Master Mason was there recognised and practiced. What is at first puzzling is that in the list of members from 1712 onwards it does not mention that these men, or any other men, received this apparent degree.

Further examination of their names, however, reveals that all of them had been at an earlier point RULERS in York, albeit, as was the traditional custom there, the titular head of the Grand Lodge was called 'President' and was, up to the 1730s, always a nobleman, whilst the actual rulers of the Grand Lodge, for day to day business, were called his Deputies but as actual rulers of a Lodge were appointed Master Masons. It is a matter of some significance that throughout the 18th century the custom in this Grand Lodge was for the Past Masters to select who should become Master Masons and by no means are all the Lodge members so invited. It was not, as is now the case, just a matter of time before one was raised to this degree. This York practice was to cause upset and division among these Brethren later but that is not a subject we can, or need to, pursue here.

It is this sense of privilege which pertains to the title 'Master Mason' which, I believe, explains how matters developed in the last instalment of this part of our story. It is Henry Sadleir, a former librarian of the Premier Grand Lodge, who tells us that in the years following 1720 a set of difficulties had to be faced as adjustments were having to be made to accommodate the latest candidates who came from the noble, military and professional classes. If, as the Premier Grand Lodge in due course stoutly proclaimed, Freemasonry consisted of 'three degrees only', that being part of the ancient triple theme to which we have referred, then those who were obligated in the existing Lodges would be aware that they were only being admitted as Fellow crafts. If these candidates had not previously been a trade apprentice then they would have to be admitted in that lower grade also. It would hardly be surprising if there would be those among the new intake who would doubtless ask: *'What about becoming a Master Mason?'*

Is it any wonder that, aware of the need to welcome as many as possible of the new potential recruits to all that Freemasonry had to offer, this Grand Lodge devised a form of Master Mason degree from the 'Second Grand Lodge' section of the Old Masonry. That included the story of the construction of Solomon's Temple as well as the commendable story of one of the Grand Masters to be involved.

When we bear in mind also that this Premier Grand Lodge did not consider the Installation of a Master a degree, and older Masonry attached the Master's Part to that step, then it begins to be clear why a so-called Master Mason's degree could be instituted which did not require of its recipient what a complete Master Mason rank had formerly demanded.

The ancient Master Mason's step that has already been shown to be in existence was so adjusted as to provide a lesser or, as some contemporaries called it, a CASUAL Master Mason degree, supplied with substituted secrets, and that not every Mason needed or wished to take. That latter provision itself shows that what was happening was a new departure, a special arrangement and a response to social demand.

This was not to be the only occasion on which our English Freemasonry would attempt to trim its sails. It can well be imagined why there were those who were disturbed at this altering of traditional procedure.

Where the setting for this lesser Master's degree comes from will be even clearer as we now turn to the next part of a search for our earlier sources. After looking at the structural elements we now think about the content.

Discovering Some Ritual Forms of Ancient Freemasonry

Once we begin to appreciate that Free and Accepted Masonry is a process that starts in the latter part of the 16th century in both England and Scotland, it is not hard to understand the fundamental source and form of all the Lodge instruction that follows.

I have just attempted to uncover the structure behind the evolving pre-1717 Lodges so as to indicate how the complete Master Mason degree had to find a new name and home as the Holy Royal Arch and its Chapters. What we must now examine is what it was that provided the bedrock of the content that makes English Freemasonry what it is.

For at least 200 years in addition to their Old Charges the members of the trade guilds of England were involved almost every year in the financing, planning and rehearsing, for their parts in a processional presentation of the biblical and folklore events from Adam at the creation of the world to God's judgment of the world at the end of time. In cities as far apart as Exeter and Newcastle-upon-Tyne, Coventry and Chester, Norwich and York many of the same scenes were enacted, in a rhymed narrative style that had to be learnt by heart, and dressed in the appropriate costume and with attendant scenery.

I was given the privilege of describing how the Masons were involved in this vivid public activity in the Prestonian Lecture for 1974, and discovered further how what they then presented related to what is still part of our ritual today.

What I now realise even more clearly 35 years on is that the whole underlying framework of our Accepted Freemasonry is the representation of the whole Bible story. If you put alongside each other the entry of the first Accepted Masons into the Guild Lodges of the latter 16th century and the fact that from 1530 onwards there is the vastly increasing publication of English language Bibles, it becomes even more evident why this link of ritual and Bible content should then occur.

What this has to do with the origin and development of the practice eventually called the Holy Royal Arch is exactly what must now be revealed.

We must start by reminding ourselves that either before the end of a present Royal Arch ceremony, or as the first act at the dining table after a meal is over, there is usually a dialogue between the MEZ and the Principal Sojourner.

The substance of this exchange is an enquiry regarding *'the three traditional Grand Lodges that we commemorate'*. What must be somewhat mystifying to today's Royal Arch Masons is why there is an enquiry at all about these bodies when there neither is, nor has been, any apparent previous reference to them. Surely the answer has to be because there was a time in the history of our Order when these Grand Lodges did actually figure as elements of our ritual that mattered.

Indeed, it may be a surprise to the Companions to recall that in the current ceremony there is a reference to the First Grand Lodge period when Moses' actions are described in conveying the Royal Arch signs. In former times, as we shall see more fully later, this Grand Lodge period figured in the Ceremony of the Veils.

The Second Grand Lodge period is briefly referred to when it is revealed that on the pillar found in the vault are the initials of the names of the three Grand Masters of that time. It was the narrative of that period that was lifted out of context to help form the present Third Degree.

The Third Grand Lodge period is the one in which we actually encounter the Grand Principals, Z., H. and J. The fact is that in the earliest days of Accepted English ritual not only did these three Grand Lodges figure much more evidently but they were not the only Grand Lodges, or eras of patriarchs, that appeared in the early catechisms.

Let me explain.

The modern Freemason has to be reminded that until at least the latter part of the 18th century there were no acted ceremonies such as a modern Freemason is accustomed to. When a candidate was introduced he was first proved, questioned as to his belief in a Supreme Being, passed around a central table and then formally admitted through the 'gates' of the Wardens and presented to the R. Wor. Master for obligation and investiture by receiving a plain apron. He was then invited to sit and take heed to the 'lectures' or catechetical questions and answers, once in verse like the mystery plays, that were conducted by the Right Worshipful Master and the Lodge members.

Catechising, may I remind the reader, was very much the fashion in the period 1530 to 1740 and in a recent book on the subject we read:

> *'The question-and-answer catechism was a most timely addition to the Protestant armoury of education and exhortation at a point when many older forms of instruction, such as wall paintings, carvings, elaborate priestly gestures and vestments, confession and religious drama were all being cast aside as*

unscriptural or denounced as idolatrous. But the catechism was seen as being much more than a simple method of imparting and acquiring information, important as that was as a starting point for the laity... Catechising would arm (them) against error and show them the paths in which they should walk to please God. In this light it is not surprising that the idea caught on and spread so quickly...' (Ian Green. The Christian's ABC. OUP. 1996. p.43)

The catechisms with which we are concerned here, as we can now see, covered the whole story of man's creation, fall and redemption, divided up into sections that show a remarkable 'rule of three'. The sections were:

Adam, Cain and Abel.
Seth, Lamech and Tubal.
Noah, Shem and Japheth.
Abraham, Isaac and Jacob.
Moses, Aholiab and Bezaleel.
Solomon, Hiram of Tyre and Hiram Abi.
Josiah, Hilkiah and Shaphan.
Zerubbabel, Haggai and Joshua.
Joseph, Mary and Jesus.
Peter, James and John.
Pilate, Caiaphas and Christ.

When we understand the Masonic tradition laid out in this way we begin to appreciate why it is that Dr Anderson, as the compiler of the first Premier Grand Lodge Constitutions, could claim even Adam as a Mason, describe the early Accepted Masons as Noachidae or sons of Noah, and Shem and Japheth as 'Masons true'.

We see how Moses, Solomon, Josiah, Zerubbabel and their Companions were honoured as princely and knightly builders or protectors of the most sacred place of worship, not only of the Jews but also, by association, of Christians.

With the New Testament characters we have the fulfilment of the Word that was recorded in John's Gospel, chap. 1. Above all, we can now appreciate afresh the significance of the Graham Ms., and, I repeat, the selection, indeed extraction, out of context, of the Second Grand Lodge events as the medium for the construction of a partial Master Mason degree. It was not just the rank of a Master Mason that was now misplaced, but the whole embryonic Master's Part, later to be given the name, Holy Royal Arch of Jerusalem, as the Mason's completing step, had to be reformulated.

The true origin of the Royal Arch was therefore long before its eventual name.

To explain more fully what has just been claimed in regard to the Graham Ms. and the new form of the Master Mason degree we need to be aware of certain crucial features in these two ceremonies.

In the Graham Ms. which, though it may have been copied in 1726, now more obviously belongs to the late 17th century or before, we have a story of the patriarch Noah being raised from a grave by his three sons, and even though their attempt experiences a 'slip' the father is clasped with the f.p.o.f. including 'hand (in) to back'.

Yet that is far from showing the relevance of this Ms. to the emergence of what will be called the Royal Arch. Here, however, appears Bazalliell (later Bezaleel) who was to teach the two sons of a king that *'without another to themselves to make a trible voice'* they were not to discover the great secret of Masonry.

That theme is repeated when we read the following: *'the master mason he teaches the trade and ought to have a trible voice in teaching of our secrets if he be a bright man'.*

And the passage continues: *'because we do believe in a Super oratory (superior) power for all tho' the 70 (the Sanhedrin) had great power yet the 11 (Apostles) had more for they chose Matthias in place of Judas'.*

It is to be noted that here a traditional custom was being followed which was to complete the lectures with events in the New Testament.

To return again to the address by Heron Lapper in 1933. He asserts that if we are looking for evidence of pre-1717 Royal Arch traces then *'What we shall go in search of is a word and a piece of tripartite symbolism that accompanies it.'*

That is surely evident in the Graham Ms as we also read:

> *What is a perfect Lodge? The centre of a true heart.*
> *How many Masons is so called? Any odd number from 3 to 13.*
> *Why so much odd and still having odd numbers?*
> *Still in reference from the blessed trinity to the coming of Christ with his 12 Apostles.*

You cannot get more New Testament than that.

Following on the all too obvious parallel between the events surrounding Noah and the story of our present third degree, it is striking to see in this Ms. that the appearance and work of Hiram is nowhere linked with withholding a secret or being in any way molested even though there is mention of some dissent between the labourers and the masons about the payment of wages.

It seems clear that by the time this Ms. was copied there had been the transfer of events to make possible a part of his story for a partial Master Mason degree. The remaining portions of a larger story are concealed or disregarded. What has to be remarked on is that the transfer of the 'grave' events from Noah to Hiram may have been to distance the Premier Grand Lodge from the old link between Noah and Jesus.

Examining afresh the 'Early Masonic Catechisms' of Knoop, Jones and Hamer, I detect some other persistent items that suggest the source of what will eventually be called the 'Royal Arch'.

The first trail involves the three Lights in the Lodge.

In the Edinburgh Register House Ms. (EHR) of 1696 we read:

'Ans (wer). The one denotes the master mason, the other the warden, The third the setter craft.'

In 1700, in the Chetwode Crawley Ms we have:

'The one Denotes the Master mason the other the Words and the Third the fellow-craft"

and in the Kevin Ms. it is exactly the same. In the Sloane Ms it is:

'(A) three, the sun, the master and the Square'.

The 'Mason's Examination' has:

'Three. the Master, Warden and Fellows' while two Catechisms in 1724 and 1725 have them representing *'Father, Son and Holy Ghost'*

and The Whole Institutions of 1724 and 1725 both have 12:

'Father, Son, Holy Ghost: Sun, Moon, Master Mason: Square, Rule, Plum: Kine, Mell & Cheisal.'

Thus, we arrive at 'A Mason's Confession' of 1727.

In answering the same question we have this:

'A. Three. Q. What are these? The south-east, south, and south-west... To be particular in showing how the master-mason stands at the south-east corner of the lodge, and the fellow-crafts next to him, and next to them the wardens, and next the entered prentices.'

From this response it is natural to come to the Wilkinson Ms. of 1725–9 and Prichard's 'Masonry Dissected' of 1730. In both these the wording regarding the lights is the same:

'The Sun to rule the Day, the Moon the Night and the Master Mason his Lodge.'

What is consistently the same is that there is, in all these extracts, the same emphasis on the 'Master Mason' as a ruler in the Lodge, even when he is replaced by one of the Holy Trinity. There are wardens, fellows and prentices but the grade of Master Mason is solitary and unique.

I find it instructive in the Edinburgh House Register Ms to read, after an explanation of the manner of making an apprentice: *'But to be a master mason... There is more to be done which after follows.'*

Sadly, it does not, but at least we know that in 1696 it was still natural to consider a Master Mason as a normal grade. Of course, there would be Past Masters but they, as these catechisms show, are bound to have been already 'through the Chair'.

Whatever the Premier Grand Lodge may have done before 1729, by this date Wilkinson and Prichard can still record the sole place of a Master Mason as that of a Harod, one of the Harodim, the overseers and controllers of Fellows. This was part of the 'ancient masonry' which contemporaries were seeing as in decline.

Another trait in these Catechisms is, of course, the distinctly Christian nature of so much of the symbolism, as when in the Dumfries Ms of 1710 we have the following Qustion and Answer regarding the Temple's inner sanctuary:

> 'What meant ye golden door of ye temple where they went into sanctum sanctorum(sic) A. It was another type of Christ who is ye door ye way and the truth & ye life by whom & in whom all ye elect entreth into heaven.'

This passage, among others, is identical with what appears in Chapter ritual at Sheffield in the 1770s. Turning now to the present opening of the third degree and thinking about the inserted, extra catechism we have another mystery. It now seems certain that this passage which begins with 'What inducement have you...?' was once part of instructive catechetical ritual that was conducted around the Lodge table.

I have already written about this matter in my recent book, *Let Me Tell You More*, but as this issue is relevant to our present study and certain new ideas have come to me since I wrote previously, I will add something else.

The very fact that this type of ritual procedure began to be dispensed with in the Craft and Royal Arch from the 1780s highlights the singularity and intriguing nature of this portion being deliberately retained.

It neither is, nor was likely to be, a normal part of the pre- or post-Union Master Mason degree and yet here it is before that degree has even begun. The only possible explanation of this arrangement has to be that this catechetical section introduced something of such importance for the Master Mason that it had to be retained somehow or other.

If this explanation is correct, however, then we are led to enquire what the important matter was that had to be brought to mind. To answer that question, however, means that we have to be absolutely clear as to what is being said in the catechism and that includes an understanding of the important initial question:

> 'What inducement have you to leave the East and go to the West?'

Various possible solutions to this question were dealt with in my longer paper elsewhere but what finally occurred to me was that if Hiram Abi was here referred to it could be the Jerusalem Temple that was the setting for this dialogue. If that was the case then how did that help to explain what was being said?

The answer was that it helped a great deal. The Temple at Jerusalem was situated along the OPPOSITE alignment to that of a present Masonic Lodge. It is in such a setting that the words of this catechism have to be understood.

They refer to a pilgrim who enters the Temple precinct via the Golden Gate in the East and proceeds to the inner temple in the West. He then enters that inner temple between the two pillars, moves into the Holy Place, where the legendary history states that Hiram Abi was slain, and his sharing in the ultimate secret was thus lost UNTIL another was chosen to take his place.

The Masonic pilgrim, however, is not meant to rest here as the present Third degree, with its substituted secrets, might suggest. The catechism rather implies that that is not the ultimate goal of this degree, for the reply to the initial query is very clear:

'To seek for THAT which is LOST which with your INSTRUCTION and our own INDUSTRY we HOPE to FIND.' (Author's emphasis)

These words deserve some careful reflection

Let me remind you that the ritual does not say *'To seek for that which is lost but which, even with your instruction we cannot hope to find, and certain substituted secrets is all we can hope to receive.'* No.

Even though 'substituted secrets' is what the Senior Warden regretfully reports at the close of this ceremony that is not what the opening catechism promises. The plainly specified objective of a Master Mason's path is that 'with the Worshipful Master's greater knowledge which he can impart', i.e. by Instruction, and the Brethren's own efforts to acquire that knowledge, it is expected that the TRUE LOST SECRET can be found.

This surely prompts the renewed question: why did the post-Union ritual composers, who knew that only substituted secrets would be found in an incomplete ceremony, take the trouble to include this old catechism in the opening of a degree they approved?

To reinforce what has already been a suggestion but is now manifestly the only conclusion, the catechism was included because the ritual formers knew that, whatever a candidate in this form of the Master Mason's degree might imagine; he had NOT completed his journey as a Mason by receiving the substituted secrets.

It might seem to some that the present Master Mason's degree may seem complete in itself but those who designed this ritual, bearing in mind what was said earlier about the true Master Mason, knew that this was not the whole story. That is why they had to include what might otherwise seem an anomaly at the outset of the ceremony but was essential for pointing candidates to what was its true end, that is now called the Holy Royal Arch. Notice also that if a candidate wants to share in the original, and total, aim of being an Accepted Master Mason then there is more than what we have here for him to experience.

Not only so but the inference is that it is only by the help of an Installed Master

Mason that this essential, additional knowledge can be gained.

What the pre-1717 Master Mason knew was the true Master's Part,which came, in a legitimate manner, with the aid of Passing the Chair.

And it is not just the opening catechism that makes the point.

Do you recall what the Worshipful Master says in the latter part of the present M. M. ceremony when he has described the disinterment of Hiram Abi?

He declares *'that that T. and W. should designate all Master Masons throughout the universe, UNTIL time and circumstances SHALL restore the GENUINE'*.

There is not the slightest question here of this degree being the end of the story. There is more that the MM after 1725, as of today, has to discover and receive.

That is why, on a Sunday afternoon in 1732, a Past Grand Master of the Premier Grand Lodge, the Revd Dr Desaguliers no less, introduced three noblemen to further secrets in a ceremony held in the Duke of Montagu's home at Thames Ditton, Surrey.

Dr Desaguliers was one of those who had laid it down that ancient Masonry consisted of three degrees and no more. So whatever he did that afternoon to make those noblemen Super Excellent Chapters must have been part of the three degrees and was, presumably, the completion of being a Master Mason.

The inducement of which mention was made earlier in this section was, as it had been from the earliest tradition of English Freemasonry, to enable our progress through the original Temple from East to West until we reach the central spot of the Holy of Holies where the full glory of the Most High is at last revealed. It was because the partial Master Mason ceremony was introduced that the remainder of the original tradition was re-presented.

It was named the Holy Royal Arch.

Moreover, in his well-known reference to the 1743 procession at Youghal in Southern Ireland, Dassigny 'clearly enunciated the noteworthy opinion, which he evidently held, that no brethren were entitled to receive this degree until, as he expressed it, they had made "a proper application, and are received with due formality; and .. it is an organised body of men who have passed the Chair, and given undeniable proofs of their skill".' (Redfern Kelly, AQC XXX. P.12)

In AQC LXX Bro. Dashwood queried the exact meaning of Dassigny's remarks as to whether in so early a period as the late 1730s the requirement of having been in a Craft Chair was a likely one. In examining further evidence even he comes to the conclusion that the original Installation was part of what we now call the Royal Arch and this further supports the subsequent view of the Antients that a Royal Arch Mason had to be someone through the Chair. That was so essential that the Moderns later required it.

Traces of an Outline Ceremony

Though he was himself totally convinced that what we know as the basic elements of the Holy Royal Arch were in existence before ever that title was used, it was nonetheless a constant claim of Bro the Revd Frederick Castells that as early as 1725 there was a clear indication that this part of Masonry existed by name.

It was in his book, *Organisation of the Royal Arch Chapter Two Centuries Ago*, that he introduced his readers to an incident mentioned in Q.C. Transactions Vol. XXI which involved a Harlequin procession supposed to have been held in that year. It was reported that in that procession the XIXth Banner displayed was that of the Royal Arch, carried by six Gentleman Masons, while two others carried 'the pageant'.

Hitherto, the earliest mention of a similar procession was that by Dr Dassigny at Youghall, Ireland 18 years later, when he described certain Excellent Masons carrying an Arch in public, and much ink was used in commenting on that revelation in the course of the last century.

What has always remained in my mind was being in the office of the Grand Scribe E of Scotland some 25 years ago and being asked what could possibly be the point of a tall, curved, iron frame that was leaning against their office wall. It gave me great delight to reveal that this was a Scottish version of just such another arch as that paraded in 1743.

The more distinctive details of the 1725 items were the fact that there was such a representative banner, whether hung from an arch or not, and hence the presence of symbolic items relating to the Royal Arch of the day.

In addition there was this 'pageant' which was almost certainly a model of the Ark of the Covenant which was carried by the two Masons grasping the ends of the two rods which ran through the rings at its side. The very appearance of this banner and model must have conjured up memories of the procession shared in during Corpus Christitide in both Eire and England a little over a century and a half previously.

Bro Castells adds the comment:

'the writer has very little to say about it; evidently he views it as a well-established Institution'. (op. cit.pp 26, 27)

He also went on to say:

'It is acknowledged that Craft Masonry (of 1717) was a movement which aimed at supplanting the Old Freemasonry; it was intended as a substitution. Whence, then, could the Royal Arch have come from? The only reasonable supposition is that the Royal Arch was substantially part of the older type of

Freemasonry which had preceded the Grand Lodge of London (and Westminster).' (p. 19)

Bro Gould, the renowned, if now hardly ever read, historian of global Masonry, long held the then usual view that the Royal Arch was a newcomer in the 1740s but even he was granted some glimpse of the truth when he reported that in the same year as the Harlequin procession (1725), three Masons – Charles Cotton Esq, Mr. Papillon Ball and Mr. Thomas Marshall – were together *'regularly pass'd Masters'*.

This puzzled him for it seemed as if there must be a further ceremony where such a practice was possible. He, of course, could not conceive that there already was a form of Masonry in which, as was obviously to be the case throughout the following century, three candidates were always to be admitted together as Royal Arch Masons when they were true Master, Masons through the Chair.

It is worth reminding readers here that in the Old American ritual, later used in Deptford near London, it was stated clearly in the obligation:

'when Candidates occupied the Chairs of the Chapter they would on no account ever exalt either more or less than three Candidates at a time'.

In the 1970s I was myself invited at a Chapter in Philadelphia to become the third candidate so that two other Americans might be able to receive Exaltation. It is also worth reminding present day Royal Arch Companions that when they are to be invested the ritual still uses the plural form even if only one person is so received.

Such is the persistence of legitimate tradition.

In our continuing search for traces and outlines of what was to be called the Royal Arch, before there was a full-blown ceremony, a paper by Bro Fulke Radice in AQC 77 gives us very useful information.

He lists 23 instances of what are likely early references to this aspect of Masonry but it is with six of them that he particularly concerns himself as being the most reliable and informative. He begins with the words of Dr Anderson, the compiler of the first Constitutions of the Premier Grand Lodge, in 1723 when he writes:

'...an annual grand Assembly wherein... the Royal Art may be duly cultivated and the Cement of the Brotherhood preserv'd; so that the whole Body resembles a well built Arch'.

How, Radice asks, did he come to use the word 'Arch' when the more natural words would have been 'edifice' or 'building'? And he continues:

'Yet Anderson, who is supposed to know nothing in 1723 about the Royal Arch, deliberately used a word which was not used anywhere else in Freemasonry, as is supposed to be the case in the first quarter of the 18th century... Whatever view we may hold of the origins of the R.A. this sentence of Anderson cannot be ignored.' (pp.205f)

If that reference was important then Radice thinks that the next mention in the 1723 Regulations has 'a very great bearing on the whole question'.

The wording is:

'The Master of a particular LODGE has the Right and Authority of congregating the Members of his LODGE into a CHAPTER at pleasure...'
(Radice's emphasis)

There were those, such as the formidable Eric Ward, who simply felt that Anderson was here reversing the medieval prohibition of operative masons forming chapters. Radice takes the point but in a long, reasoned and well-argued passage insists that if that was what Anderson was really doing then why did Grand Master Payne still insist that this power of a Master be reaffirmed.

Bro Radice, in particular, refers to the early minutes of the Old King's Arms Lodge No. 29, where that Lodge did meet as a Chapter for a different form of business. As a further argument for the idea of some form of Royal Arch working in the 1720s, Bro Radice mentions a Book E in which we read:

'This day (it was 1721) the Free Masons of London, in the name of themselves and the rest of their Brn. of England, vested their Separate and Distinct rights and powers of Congregating in Chapters, etc... in the present old Lodges...'

We next have our attention directed to a Dublin catechism of 1725, 'The Whole Institution of Free-Masons Opened', where it is stated:

'Yet for all this I want the primitive Word. I answer it was God in six terminations, to wit I am, and JOHOVAH is the answer to it... for proof read the first of the first of St. John.' (Early Masonic Catechisms p.88)

Of this Radice says that it surely needs no further comment, as also of two extracts from a 1726 newspaper advertisement in which there is mention of 'a Rule of Three' and 'movable Letters' used in a ceremony.

The Graham Ms. and the activity of Dr Desaguliers in Surrey in the 1730s have already been mentioned and those who want to follow up the other references here know where to go.

It would be unhelpful for the new student of these matters if we did not refer at this point to three aspects of Masonry being practiced in the capital between 1735 and 1745 as well as one feature of English North Country Masonry. What has to be commented on from the outset is the peculiar fact that, whatever may, or may not, have been the significance of these practices for revealing how the presence of some form of Masonry later called 'Royal Arch' was around at this date, when a more deliberate presence and practice of the Royal Arch makes its appearance in England, these Southern activities all disappear.

It is just as if, having done their task of keeping alive essential features of 'old Masonry', they can now fade away because a true and legitimate practice has resurfaced. That is a phenomenon which has been often noted but, I dare to believe, never been adequately appraised and examined. What were these activities really saying to Freemasonry in its new Premier Grand Lodge guise?

I turn first to the acknowledged presence in the new 1730s Masters Lodges of a body of men known as Scots Masters.

Bernard Jones tells us that the 'Scots Master' is mentioned in the minutes of some Lodges in the 1730s and thereabouts; for example, in the minutes of an old Bath Lodge we learn that *'the Lodge of Masters met Extraordinary & our worthy Brothers were made & admitted SCOTS MAS(te)r MASONS'*. This minute is typical of a number. (Freemasons' Guide p.255)

Bro Jones goes on to tell us in his *Book of the Royal Arch* that the members of this degree claimed to possess *'the true history, secret and design of Freemasonry, and to hold various privileges'* so that, whilst there remains some mystery about them it is likely that it was a preliminary to either the Royal Arch or the Mark or both.

He certainly accepts that such Masons existed and clearly fitted into the area between the Craft Third Degree, the Mark and the eventual Royal Arch.

From what we learn of these Scots Masters from other sources their relevance to our present subject is clear. (op.cit.p.40)

Other occasional writers and commentators on this subject in Quatuor Coronati Transactions together give us at least some idea of how these Scots Masters fitted into the contemporary scene.

They were regular attenders at Masters' Lodges and always sat in the East on the right of the Worshipful Master. They wore hats, as a mark of their Past Master status, and they had a wide red sash from which hung a miniature buckler. They were known to lay claim to knowledge superior to that of even the ordinary Past Master and their presence in Lodges of such Masons was so as to witness to the further progress that a Mason had yet to make for the completion of his journey.

In 1971, Bro Harry Carr, the renowned Secretary and Editor of Quatuor Coronati Lodge, published his book on Early French Exposures and in the section entitled 'Le Parfait Maçon' the following further information is provided:

> *'It is said among the Masons, that there are still several degrees above that of the masters... Those called ECOSSAIS (or Scots, but not Scottish) claim that they form the fourth grade... Instead of weeping over the ruins of the Temple of Solomon, as their brethren do, the ECOSSAIS are concerned with rebuilding it ... It is from (that) great event that the ECOSSAIS derive the epoch of their institution, & although they are later than the other Masons by several centuries, they consider themselves of a superior grade. The following is the basis on which their pre-eminence is founded. When the question arose of rebuilding the Temple of the Lord, Zerubabel (sic) chose from the three grades of Masonry*

the most capable workmen but due to disruptions caused by the Samaritans this Prince (took) the precaution of creating a fourth grade of Masons, whose number he limited to 753, chosen from among the most excellent artists; these not only supervised all the others, but they were also charged with watching the security of the workmen ... they were also awarded a more favourable rate of pay.'

It is interesting to note that at just this date Dassigny reports that in York there were some Master Masons who received higher pay.

Bearing in mind that the passwords of a Master Mason in this form of Masonry were *'Adonai Schilo'* the words of a Scots Master were *'Schilo, Shelomeh abif'* (meaning, Son of the Lord, Solomon my father).

There then follows the residue of the many questions that were in the original ceremony. What is left is remarkable:

Are you a ECOSSAIS Master?
I was brought out of the captivity of Babylon.
Who honoured you with the degree of ECOSSAIS?
Prince Zerubabel, of the line of David and Solomon.
When?
Seventy years after the destruction of the holy city.
In what are the ECOSSAIS Masons occupied?
In rebuilding the Temple of God.
Why do the ECOSSAIS Masons carry the sword and the buckler?
In memory of the order given by Nehemiah to all the workmen ... to have swords always at their sides, & their bucklers near at hand during work, for use in case of attack by their enemies.
How was the new Temple built?
On the foundations of that of Solomon, & according to his plans..."

It is not without interest or relevance that the reader should know that the biblical figures that are associated with the various grades in this working of 'Le Parfait Maçon' are: Apprentice, Adam; Fellow, Noah; Master, Solomon; and the name of a Master Mason is given as 'Harodim'.

In the light of what was said above it should be noted that one meaning of Harodim is 'supervisors'.

At a little earlier date (1740) than the above, there were in Spitalfields, London, at least two Lodges that worked a ceremony entitled 'Le Rite du Bouillon'.

For those who may ever have wondered what a 'completed' Master Mason degree could have looked like, this example is the nearest that I have ever encountered and, thanks to a copy of their ceremony carefully preserved in the United Grand Lodge library, I here present some portions of that working.

It begins with a significant Introduction:

'King Solomon employed a great many workmen of the surrounding nations to build the Holy Temple of Jerusalem, and he imparted unto them, as well as to his own people the Israelites, the mysteries of the Craft … But in process of time, Kings and Princes desired to learn the mysteries of this ancient Society … so that the Order passed ALMOST OUT OF THE HANDS of its first holders into those of NOBLE and GENTLE birth … But it was not until Godefroy de Bouillon delivered Jerusalem, that the brethren of this ancient society perceived how far they had DEPARTED from ORIGINAL simplicity and truth;. … it was found that certain strange things had CREPT INTO the mysteries, which were never done nor heard of at Jerusalem. … so that the return of the Crusaders introduced once more into Europe the PURE & SIMPLE mysteries of Jerusalem and they are these which have been preserved even until now.' (My emphases to show parallels with what was then current English development.)

The candidate is now told that there are three degrees and *'in the Master Mason's degree the Master represents King Solomon of Israel, the Senior Warden King Hiram of Tyre, and the Junior Warden represents Hiram Abiff the skilful workman, the Treasurer represents Adoniram and the Secretary… Joabert.'*

The Master takes his seat in the East *'and because he can have no superior, he must remain covered'* (wear a hat).

The candidate *"shall then be clothed in a white robe (for the Latin 'candidus' means 'white') reaching down to his ankles, and bound round the waist with a girdle."*

The similarity to a monk is not out of place.

When it comes to the Investiture of an Apprentice the Junior Warden says:

"I… present to you a White Lambskin Apron, the original garment that our Almighty Father presented to our first parents after their fall. It is a Badge the most ancient as well as the most honourable, for while it reminds us that we are members of a fallen race, it also teaches us that by the sacrifice of the lamb, we are clothed with innocence." (op.cit. pp. 15ff)

I mention these passages as reminding us of the way in which in ancient Masonry the whole Bible story from Adam's fall to Christ's saving work was intended to be told.

Passing through the Fellow-craftsman to the Master's Degree we are told that

'the Master of the Lodge is robed in scarlet, and crowned so as to represent King Solomon of Israel, The Senior Warden in robes of purple, and crowned as Hiram, King of Tyre, and the Junior Warden in plain black and flowing garments as Hiram Abiff.'

A note on this page tells us that in the frontispiece to the Constitutions of the

Antients Grand Lodge (Ahiman Rezon), Moses, Aholiab and Bezaleel, Z., H. and J. are all shown wearing similar clothing.

The Junior Deacon not only acts as conductor but also acts at some points as a candidate, *'a less number than three not being eligible'*.

We recall what was said about this at an earlier point: *"Should there be only one Candidate for this degree, another brother must take part with the Junior Deacon to complete the number. The Lodge is opened as a Fellow-Craft Lodge but the Senior Warden retires immediately after.'*

We now pass to the moment when 'Three Craftsman from the quarries. . seek an audience, at the suggestion of the Grand Master Hiram Abiff, from our Sovereign Lord King Solomon.'

The Junior Deacon now states their case:

> *'The Temple being now finished and dedicated to the true and ever-living God (sic), whose name be exalted, we are anxious to obtain that great reward graciously promised unto us, of being admitted unto the honourable degree of Geometric Master Mason'.*

To which the WM replies:

> *'Brethren, the cause of the delay which you have experienced proceeds from the absence of our Royal friend and ally, King Hiram of Tyre ... If ye are however willing to take upon yourselves the obligation of a Master Mason, and await the return of our Royal ally, we may thus far hasten your admission.'*

The complete Obligation (op.cit.p.25) cannot here be given but it includes the specific mention of the 10 Commandments and the F.P.O.F. as well as the very words to be used in the degree later known as The Secret Monitor in which the candidate will *'sooner advise when in difficulty, instruct him when ignorant, succour him when afflicted and apprise him of all approaching danger if in my power to do so.'*

He swears, also, not to reveal the *'Grand Mysterious Word of a Geometric Master Mason, which I shall hereafter receive.'* The Master then gives these brethren a Hailing Sign and the Word ZABULON which means "Eternal Habitation' and when joined with JEHOVAH naturally describes the presence of Shekinah in the Holy of Holies, the spot where the Divine sometimes comes to dwell.

Having seen the word ZABULON used in a number of early Chapter documents in the Flanders area of that period I wonder if we have mistaken Jabulon for a rendering of this term. It is a matter to which we must return before this journey ends.

The Lodge having reassembled after refreshment the Junior Warden absents himself. The Junior Deacon with the candidates approaches the Master and again requests the granting of the rank of Geometric Master Mason, at which the WM asks: *'Where is our worthy Grand Master Hiram Abiff?'* to which the Senior Deacon replies: *'Sire, when we retired from labour to refreshment at high meridian, he remained behind … He may yet be at his devotions.'*

Emphasising once more, as with King Hiram, the 'Rule of Three', the WM says: *'We shall not proceed without him'* at which a search is started for the Third Grand Master. In the preparation room they find the Junior Warden on his back, in a grave, with a sprig of evergreen at his head. On hearing the news King Solomon declares this to be Hiram, for he had heard that two fellow-Craftsmen had demanded the Master Mason secrets which Hiram could not give them because he had *'entered into a covenant with the King of Tyre not to reveal the same in his absence…'*

The Senior Warden now expresses his fear that the *'most sacred and mysterious word may be lost'* but the WM says: *'I hope not, my Brother. We permitted him, it is true, after the casting of the pillars of J- and B-, to engrave the most mysterious word upon a plate of gold within the cabalistic figure of our signet, and to wear it as an especial mark of our royal favour and goodwill, and I doubt not that it remains with him.'*

So they proceed to the grave where Hiram lies as a corpse. The brethren are asked to take the shoulders and the feet to lay him on the ground when the WM and Senior Warden take the appropriate grip and raise him up. The Master then puts his hand into the Junior Warden's bosom and takes out a gold medal wherein are interlaced triangles within a circle and the Tetragrammaton in the centre. The Master and Warden kiss the medal and then return to the Lodge.

The Master carries the Jewel above his head until he reaches the Bible when he removes the square and compasses and replaces them with the medal. He then says:

> *'Brethren how fortunate are you in having recovered this jewel. Upon it is engraved the most mysterious Word. . These four letters compose the Tetragrammaton, which is the name of the only true and living God. He in his mercy deigned to reveal the name to Enos (Enoch), and unto Jacob, and unto Moses, and it has descended unto us from our great grandsire B-, through Obed and Jesse, even by the lips of our father David, of ever memorable memory . . and we did in solemn conclave communicate it to King Hiram and Hiram Abiff. We so write it that no one can pronounce it but he who receives it from living lips.'*

The candidates then formed themselves into groups of three in which they whispered the Grand Word and the Mysterious Word. The Master concluded by pointing out that the six points of the interwoven triangles indicated the SIX points of Fellowship ending with *'mouth to ear to warn each other'*.

But there is also the cabbalistic interpretation:

> *'The erect triangle is a symbol of God in his justice, the inverted one God in his mercy; the circle is eternity, without beginning and without end. God is the beginning, medium and end of all things, to whom be benediction, and*

honour, and glory, and power, and dominion for ever and ever. Amen.'

They are now invested with the apron (not described), given the working tool of a Master Mason, which is a trowel to *'unite Brother unto Brother by the cement of brotherly love'*.

The candidates are also taught a Geometric alphabet or cypher that is drawn on the trestle board.

Finally, the Master describes how the word was lost by the invasion of the Assyrians and not recovered until St. John revealed it in his Epistle. There he described how the true pronunciation was lost in the exile at Babylon and ADONAI was substituted. The final revelation was on Mount Tabor as Moses and Elijah appeared with Jesus to Peter, James and John, and Jesus explained his name: I AM ALPHA AND OMEGA.

This was not known to the other disciples until after the Resurrection. Here also was revealed *'that great and glorious NAME'* which, in our present Royal Arch working, is only made privy to the First Principal.

So ended the Rite du Bouillon. It will again be noted how so much of the whole Bible story was recalled.

It is hardly surprising that the Premier Grand Lodge, on discovering the nature of this working, not only forbade its members to attend these Lodges but declared its teaching irregular and misleading. What is intriguing is that not only did the coffin of the dead Hiram Abiff bear the letters of the Tetragrammaton in the Prichard exposure of the third degree but to this day the Master Mason ceremony in the Netherlands has the same decoration on the coffin.

In both these cases there is no explanation offered to a candidate of this significant and holy name. Why should that be? Was it because there was ignorance of its meaning? Was it because this was knowledge not to be shared with the new Master Masons and reserved for Grand Officers or those through the Chair? Or was it because this was being taught in Lodges that did not owe their allegiance to the Premier Grand Lodge?

The fact remains that presented with the nearest one could come to a Third Degree that WAS able to be complete in itself and with no substituted secrets the Premier Grand Lodge turned its back and those of its brethren on such a rite. Is it any wonder that there were those Masons who began to discover that there was more to be known in Masonry and would take steps to make it available.

In nothing is this more clear than in the Masonic ceremonies of the late 1730s than those known as the 'Heredom of Kilwinning' and which were revived, not in Scotland as would have been expected, but in London.

As this form of Freemasonry is still actively pursued by knowledgeable brethren today, and I have savoured it for almost 50 years, one cannot be as free with its content as in the Rite just revealed.

However, since what is otherwise called 'The Royal Order' has so much to do with preserving Old St John Masonry, and especially the parts that we now call the Holy Royal Arch, we must mention four of its features. What is more we shall see later in this book that the first three features are found to be identical 30 years later in forms of English Chapter working.

The first remarkable fact is that in a rhyming form of catechetical instruction between the Ruler and Past Rulers of what is called a Provincial CHAPTER there is laid out for the candidates the whole Masonic meaning of the biblical story from the books of Genesis to Revelation. The idea mentioned earlier of various patriarchal epochs is here displayed.

The second feature is that as the catechisms embody the whole range of usual issues taught in English Lodges – what are the reasons for 9, 7, 5 and 3; the three great principles; why the Ark, Mount Moriah and the Middle Chamber – they are also shown to have their ultimate fulfilment in the Christian dispensation. The third feature is expressed in the following dialogue just before the Chapter closes:

> *Since opening the Chapter what have we been doing?*
> *Seeking a Word which was lost, and which by your assistance we have now found. (An echo from the third degree opening?)*
> *When was the Word lost?*
> *The Word was lost unto the sons of men, when the Saviour descended to the infernal den.*
> *When was the Word found?*
> *When he triumphant rose, o'er Sin and Death, our sempiternal foes.*

The fourth feature is the subsequent meeting of a Provincial Grand Lodge known as an assembly of the Rosy Cross.

In this meeting the representative candidate (for there are normally several in attendance) mentally assents to an obligation with a sword in one hand and a trowel in the other. The difficulties facing the Jews returning from Babylon are rehearsed and the foregoing stance was therefore adopted:

> *'One hand the Sword against the foe did shake*
> *The other hand the Trowel up did take.*
> *Oh, valiant minds, lo, here's a worthy part,*
> *The Jews quailed not at ruin of their wall,*
> *But champion-like, improved Freemasons' art.'*

In this ceremony the candidates thus become Knights of the Rosy Cross and it is doubtless from this early association of what we can begin to discern as a form of Royal Arch practice that there derives the association with Masonic knighthood.

It may seem odd but out of Jewish warriors come Christian ones. It is in this 1730–1750 period, as attempts are made to preserve or revive pre-1717 elements of what was called St John's Masonry, that the main features of what was called the Holy Royal Arch of Jerusalem clearly emerge.

What must now occupy us are the following questions. Why, when it was evident that the sublime conclusion of Accepted Freemasonry was being neglected or sidelined, was no serious effort made to repair the process? Why, moreover, in the light of these reproductions of much older practice, did the Premier Grand Lodge continue to be so opposed to the Royal Arch?

Why did the Premier Grand Lodge avoid the Royal Arch for 50 Years?

As more general historians begin to be aware of the contribution that Freemasonry can make to social studies they might well be surprised to discover that our Fraternity is a rather more complex organisation than they at first imagined.

What they will discover is a system that includes more than the three basic degrees.

They will have to cope with aspects such as the Mark, the Royal Arch and Knights Templar. Such thinking started me off on a new line of study.

It is, of course, hardly surprising that the historians should have had a shock. They would learn that the Scottish and Irish Grand Lodges still claim that their Freemasonry consists of three degrees only and for half a century after the formation of the 1717 London and Westminster or Premier Grand Lodge, the Freemasonry of that body was stated by its leaders to be composed of only three degrees.

Even in 1761, their Grand Secretary gave expression to this Grand Lodge's position by informing an Irish supplicant for charity that *'We are neither Arch* (that was a completion of the Mark degrees), *Royal Arch nor Antient'*.

That was the flag under which the Premier Grand Lodge was sailing at that time. That must have seemed quite clear and straightforward.

Yet it is also a fact that whilst the Premier Grand Lodge took up this position there was evidence around that ancient Freemasonry consisted of more than what was revealed in those three degrees. There were, we are told, even some Moderns Masons who practiced the Royal Arch in some form.

Why was that truth not acknowledged?

Was it, for example, as I was told early on in the Craft, that it was simply a case of rivalry between the Premier Grand Lodge and the Grand Lodge of the Antients?

That would seem to be an easy solution but it then leaves serious questions to be answered.

The Antients Grand Lodge only appears in 1751 so one has to ask what prompted the Premier Grand Lodge's view in the years before that? Moreover, the most recent Batham Lecturer has claimed that the Antients did not at once highlight any practice of the Royal Arch, so that an argument for difference on that score becomes even weaker. And there must also have been sound reasons why some Masons felt that an alternative to the existing Grand Lodge was necessary. This leads us to the query, 'how old is the Royal Arch'?

Contrary to most previous opinions, and as I have already sought to show, I believe that what we call the Royal Arch originated quite some time BEFORE its present NAME began to be used. What emerged in the 1720s was what was called the 'Casual Master Mason', or our present Master Mason degree, that was not as adequate as that of a true, or Geometric, Master Mason.

Put simply, the complete and authentic grade of Master Mason was one that embodied three other elements which are manifestly missing in our present third degree but which find expression in what we now call the Royal Arch.

The three elements were, and still are:

1. *The discovery of the True Mason Word as God's full revelation of Himself.*
2. *The 'rule of three', or Chair degrees, by which the Word is preserved and communicated.*
3. *The recognition of God's people returning from the exile in Babylon in order to build a new Temple in Jerusalem.*

All these elements are known to have existed in Masonic usage well before the name Royal Arch was ever adopted to describe and continue their use.

It is against this background that I again pose the question: *"Why then did the Premier Grand Lodge avoid the Royal Arch for 50 years?"*

It seems to me that there are three possible areas in which we might find a solution. Each of these areas reveals the differing viewpoints of those involved in the changing situations in which they found themselves. My suggestion is that it was the combined influence of these attitudes that led the Premier Grand Lodge to adopt the position it did.

The first area for investigation may perhaps be described as 'the basis of allegiance'.

What members of the 1717 Grand Lodge had to decide from the beginning was who really belonged to, or had the most proper right to determine, what was described as 'Ancient Masonry'?

In days gone by this matter would seem to have been one that concerned simply the senior members who knew the traditions of the Guild stonemasons or those who eventually joined them as Free and Accepted Masons.

Nowadays, we are much more aware of the political issues which affected those who were also very much men as well as Masons. As the new London and Westminster Grand Lodge started to consider the kind of Craft which it wanted to create the current issues of religious and political concern had to be taken into account.

In 1715, there had been distinct signs of Jacobite unrest and anyone familiar with York Freemasonry in that year knows that allegiance to the Stuart succession was a factor causing a divisive element in Craft membership there.

For anyone aware of this kind of influence, as were those who were shortly to be the leaders of the Premier Grand Lodge, there were lessons to be learnt. The Masons were aware of the Royal Society rules about no discussions of politics or religion in its meetings. But there was more that determined the attitudes of the Grand Lodge rulers.

If admitting 'Ancient Masonry' meant allowing controversial instruction from Scotland, Ireland or even York, there would need to be caution. To eliminate political and religious division in the Craft was also an urgent priority for other reasons. It was because that was required by a Government that sanctioned their existence. Anything that might savour of undue outside or foreign influence would be suspect.

There was also something else.

In late 17th century York and Chester some working stonemasons began to be displeased with the Old Guild's unsatisfactory representation of their trade. They took steps to remedy the situation by renouncing their support of their older Guilds and forming new ones with allied crafts such as bricklayers and smiths.

What is interesting is that something similar occurred in London. It would now appear that the reason why Christopher Wren, who was admitted a Free and Accepted Mason in 1663, renounced this membership in 1715 was because he too questioned the authenticity of the body that was now to claim the right to organise Freemasonry in London. His main allegiance was to the working craft. He began to have real doubts about this Free and Accepted form.

The issue that thus had to be faced by the new Grand Lodge was how a proper Tradition might be determined and how, when agreeably defined, could it be accepted and applied?

We know that these were matters that not only much exercised the minds of the members of the 1717 Grand Lodge, but that certain steps were taken to try and resolve these essential issues.

The Grand Master in 1718 and 1720, Bro George Payne, drew the attention of Grand Lodge members to the existence of those Time Immemorial documents known as 'The Old Charges' and produced one of them that had been used in 17th century Chester for a Guild Lodge.

Because of its provenance, this, he said in effect, is something that cannot be overlooked if we want to determine Tradition. Accordingly, requests for similar material were issued and when Anderson first wrote up the Grand Lodge Constitutions in 1722 he referred to them as 'The Old Constitutions' and added that they are *'Taken from a Manuscript wrote about Five Hundred Years since'*.

That claim was giving 100 years more Tradition to them than even the most ambitious student would today.

In 1723, the Revd John Theophilus Desaguliers, another Past Grand Master, wrote a preface to the first edition of the Constitutions in which he said this:

> *'I need not tell your GRACE what Pains our learned AUTHOR has taken in compiling and digesting this Book from the old Records ... still preserving all that was truly ancient and authentick in the old ones.'*

But how did he, as a new Free and Accepted Mason, know what was really authentic? Whilst we thus appreciate the group's stated desire to continue what could properly be regarded as Tradition there were three obstacles to the achieving of their aim.

The first was that access to some of the older material was prevented because members of some old Lodges who disapproved of what the new Grand Lodge intended, wilfully destroyed their manuscripts.

A second was the failure of some amongst the founding members to be able to recall exactly how some parts of the previous working went.

A third obstacle was an apparent determination by some of the Grand Lodge members to urge what they conceived to be the best form of practice regardless of what others claimed was the traditional form.

The political and religious correctness of the day revealed its influence as the brethren argued with each other as to what was the Tradition that was to be kept. Some wanted to omit parts of that Tradition that would be called the Holy Royal Arch of Jerusalem.

The second area in which a Grand Lodge group relationship operated ought best to be described as

'the issue of social distinction'.

Justifiable as the claim is that Freemasonry in so many ways is, and was meant to be, a great social leveller in which, as Scots Masons still say in their ritual: *'we all meet upon the level and part upon the square'*.

Yet, the facts are that there constantly have been, and still are, distinctions not only of Masonic but of social rank in our Craft practice. In the course of my own more recent researches in early York and Chester Freemasonry two clear examples of such social distinction have revealed themselves.

Let me explain.

As was mentioned earlier, a new Chester Masons Trade Guild separated in 1680 from the earlier Guild there and so created a new situation for the old Guild Lodge members.

By what authority did the Old Guild members now meet and to what authority could they look for reliable guidance concerning their practices?

As, among other factors, the son of one of their members, Bro George Payne, mentioned earlier, was a Past Grand Master in the Premier Grand Lodge, it was to that body that these Chester Free and Accepted Masons were directed in 1721 for authentication and advice.

One piece of advice that they much needed was how they might manage their large and growing membership. They felt that they were too unwieldy a Lodge to conduct affairs well and so they sought counsel of a highly placed Brother, the Duke of Richmond. His advice was prompt and revealing. I recommend, he said, that you at once divide into three Lodges; one Lodge for the nobility, gentlemen and the military; one for professional men and businessmen; and one for any in the menial trades, including any working masons.

That is what happened.

If you look in the book that is frequently a source of invaluable information, *Lane's List of Lodges*, – you will see that the first Lodges mentioned in Chester are the three that were so created.

Social distinction, even in the fraternal Craft, was the group's response to the management of its future. The dynamics of the Chester situation led to such a conclusion.

In York, the same picture is revealed but with a different outcome. In 1726, the Grand Lodge of All England at York held its annual Installation Festival on the Feast of St John the Baptist in June, in the same manner and as it had always done from the start of the century at least.

Following worship in one of that city's churches there was a public procession that included the Town Waits, a band of musicians and singers, and this was followed by the Installation ceremony itself and then a public banquet to which non-Masons were invited and at which speeches were made. One of these was by a Grand Warden, a certain medical doctor, Francis Drake. In his notable address this well-known local figure made the following distinctions.

He first addressed the stonemasons who were members, reminding them that the Lodge to which they now belonged was not, as in days past, just linked to their ancient trade. He then referred to the business and professional members and pointed out their particular skills and duties. And finally he addressed the gentlemen and those of noble birth in the Lodge emphasising their special responsibilities and privileges.

In York, however, there was no invitation to divide and form separate bodies but equally there was no pretence made that all those present were of the same status. The group reaction here was that of brotherly support in relation to the particular qualities of each group's background. I have to tell you that subsequent events were to test this group relationship severely, but that is another story.

What I am suggesting that we understand by these examples is that at just the point at which the Premier Grand Lodge was finding its feet there was a social atmosphere in which the recognition of different boundaries existed.

Why is it, not only in London but also in York, that the principal positions in their Grand Lodges were either from the outset, or very soon after, filled by members of the titled class? This was not a coincidence. It was determinate policy.

It was in this kind of setting that we have to see the principal members of this Grand Lodge wrestling with the existence in their midst of a contentious social issue. How were they going to manage what was as much a social reality in London and Westminster as it was in Chester and York?

In whose hands was authority to lie? Were distinctions of class to have any weight in the conduct of their affairs? How were their conclusions on any of these matters to be framed for their successors in the future?

In the light of what was said earlier about the decisions made regarding the antiquity of the Craft it is interesting to note what happened here. The first four meetings of the Grand Lodge having been presided over by Masons from the pre-Grand Lodge era such as Sayer and Payne, or that distinctive new member of the Craft, the Revd John Theophilus Desaguliers, the Grand Mastership was assumed from 1721 by peers of the realm, a practice that has continued from that day to this.

Whether by the influence of the few, or by the general consent of the new Grand Lodge assembled, the place of the nobility as properly at the head of the Craft is accepted as the norm.

Whilst that had manifestly not been the custom in the old days of working Freemasonry, it was now the form which the new groups in Masonry felt to be appropriate.

What is more, the post of Deputy Grand Master, which begins in 1720, is allocated to those who may rightly claim to be of professional or social distinction.

I merely mention Dr John Desaguliers, Martin Folkes, William Cowper, Sir Cecil Wray and the 1st Viscount Dudley and Ward. Social status was accepted as a natural guide to the choice of those who should lead in the governing of the Craft.

What is true of the personnel in Grand Lodge is also true of its first regulations. Whilst it seems to have been accepted from the outset that those Lodges that sought to set themselves under the governance of the Premier Grand Lodge were to be left undisturbed in their practice of Initiating members, and even of admitting such new members to the fresh degree of Apprentice where necessary, there was no such freedom in regard to forming new Lodges or installing the Masters of Lodges.

Here, the officers of the Premier Grand Lodge claim the right to determine both the nature of each Lodge and the suitability of its Master. Nor was this at first simply a case of paperwork. So long as it was physically feasible it seems that the Grand Master, or someone appointed as a deputy, should attend on the occasion of both a Lodge's inauguration and the first installing of a Worshipful Master.

A very real need for social proprieties to be observed seems to be a feature of the way the group operates at this stage. Above all there was to be a recognition of what was, and was not, acceptable for Lodges to practise.

It is precisely at this point that we come to the third area of our study.

When the Premier Grand Lodge, and especially its appointed officers, had begun to define the nature of what they considered the 'Ancient Craft' and to claim their right to regulate such practice we come to what might be described as the 'area of ritual definition'.

What we have to deal with here is that known portion of older Masonic practice mentioned earlier, the grade of Master Mason.

The first Grand Master after 1717, Anthony Sayer, a bookseller, was clearly stated to be a Master Mason and yet the Grand Lodge does not seem then to have wanted to make that grade available to the generality of the members. What were the factors that decided how this matter would be played?

If, as I am now convinced, the Master Mason grade was originally to be restricted to those who had been through the Chair of a Lodge then there were only three options open to the leaders of the new 1717 Craft.

One was to admit that whilst there were meant to be only three degrees, one of these as in ancient days, was a step that was restricted to rulers, either officers of the Grand Lodge or Lodge Masters.

The second option was to forego that earlier restriction and to admit a Fellow Craft to the degree called Master Mason. A very modern example of this sort of decision is to open the Chairs in the Holy Royal Arch to any Companion who, though not a Craft Worshipful Master, is considered fit to proceed to those 'mysteries and privileges'.

However, there was a third option and that was to retain the TITLE of the third degree and to allow SOME of the traditional history and purposes of the Master Mason grade to be conferred on a Fellow Craft but keeping its complete secrets for chosen Masons of noble, Grand Lodge or Past Master rank.

That this was appropriately done by Dr Desaguliers for three noblemen on a Sunday afternoon in 1735 we have already seen. Their names, interestingly, were St John, Albemarle and Russell, which is proof enough of their status.

If the Grand Lodge was right in insisting that Ancient Tradition consisted of three degrees only, even excluding the ceremony of Installation, then either Dr Desaguliers was wholly out of order in doing what he did or he was quite properly conferring the normally restricted part of a whole Master's degree.

It is not surprising that given the group relationships in the Premier Grand Lodge they would want to resist any other Tradition that was claiming to be a proper conclusion to the Master Mason degree, especially when such an end was still recognised in contemporary Irish, York or French Freemasonry.

Equally, the view prevailed that whilst men of social standing might well not enjoy being 'mere craftsmen' and might at least value the title of Master Mason, any of noble birth or superior office could be further honoured by an older 'secret distinction'.

To admit the credentials of what was now to be another degree was something to be publicly resisted as long as possible. It took the likes of a royal offspring such as Thomas Dunckerley, making the case for the Royal Arch, for change to be called for.

Only so could a Grand Secretary be made to alter his tune. With political issues on the wane social and cultural influence had the last word. What had previously blocked recognition of the Holy Royal Arch now became the reason for its acceptance, even if still reluctantly, as part of Ancient Masonry.

The Antients Grand Lodge and the Holy Royal Arch

It is now generally admitted to have been the case that there were, from at least 1730, a growing number of Freemasons who objected to the changes, or new practices, introduced under the Premier Grand Lodge of 1717.

As Bro Cyril Batham says in his collected papers on the Antients:

> 'By the middle of the 18th century, discontent within the Craft was widespread and something like a quarter of its lodges had ceased to meet, the result of disillusionment and frustration…. and thus they formed a body of opposition.'
> (Freemasonry in England and France. 1993. p.83)

The mere facts of frustration and disappointment about the conduct of matters considered to be of some consequence to Masonic brethren do not of themselves add up to anything significant unless they are directed by a determined group.

It was Bro Sadleir, Librarian to the Premier Grand Lodge, who in 1887 pointed to the likely truth of what then took place. Up to the time that he wrote the generally accepted view of the mid-century schism was that the Ancients (sic) first made an appearance in 1746. His view was of something different:

> 'Most of us are probably aware that ten years make a considerable slice in the life of an individual, but in that of a lodge or society it is quite a different matter. For my own part I firmly believe that the true origin of the 'Ancients' dates from the period of occurrence just mentioned, the end of 1735, and that they were probably countenanced and assisted by some few of the old school or poorer class of English Masons who had either dropped out from the regular lodges or had never acknowledged the authority of the Grand Lodge of 1717, but the real organisers and supporters – the head and backbone of the 'Ancient' fraternity for first 20 or 30 years of its existence – were Irish Masons.' (AQC. Vol.85. 1972.p. 187)

I cannot resist here the suggestion of an answer where, in that same article where he lists the Irish members of the Antients oldest Lodge, No. 2, he was puzzled by the name Samuel Quay heading the list.

Names that begin with QU are invariably those of Manxmen and I am firmly of the opinion that he would be a son of that island along with his fellow Celts. In the 17th century they still spoke Manx which is closely related to Gaelic Erse.

What is important in the light of Bro Sadleir's discovery is that these first Antients come from a setting in which the Royal Arch was already a separate and worked degree as is testified to by the English regimental lodges, with a warrant from the Irish Grand Lodge, who practised it and took it to Fredericksburg, USA where its first recorded usage was minuted in 1752.

For any who get excited by this, the following passage from Bro Bernard Jones needs pondering:

> 'The first official reference to the Royal Arch Degree is in the 'Antients' minutes of 1752. The Grand Committee had met at the Griffon Tavern, Holborn, London, on March 4 that year with John Gaunt, Master of Lodge No.5 in the chair and Dermott acting for the first time as Grand Secretary. It is the second meeting recorded in the minute book. It records a complaint "that (John) Macky was an Empiric in phisic: and (with Thomas Phealon) both impostors in Masonry. That upon examining some brothers whom they pretend to have made Royal-Archmen, the parties had not the least Idea of the secret. That Dr.Macky … (had not) the least Idea or knowledge of Royal Arch Masonry. But instead he had told the people whom he deceived, a long story about 12 marble stones &c and that the Rain Bow was the Royal Arch, with many other absurdities equally foreign and Ridiculous …" (op.cit.p.59.) The two Masons were banned from attending or joining any Antients Lodge for life.'

Yet the question that has persistently occupied me during most of my many years of Masonic membership is why, when some serious opposition to the Premier Grand Lodge at last came into existence from 1751, there was not an immediate turning back of the clock and the reintroduction of some third degree that more correctly represented Old English Masonry.

What is even more interesting is the fact that in nothing that I have been aware of has there been any similar query in what has been written about this portion of the 18th century. I want in the first section of this chapter to explore this question in the hope that there may at last be an answer, or the ground to be so cleared that a student of the future may supply a definitive solution.

In my pondering on this matter it has seemed that there could possibly be three reasons why more drastic change was not sought when this new Grand Lodge according to the Old Constitutions, which we now refer to as the Antients, was being established.

The first reason may have been a plain sense of realism. By 1751, the Master Mason degree which was accredited by the Premier Grand Lodge had been 'in situ' for 25 years. It was not yet a normal step of progression for most Masons and it was certainly not looked upon, as it is today, as an inevitable part of progress in one's own Lodge. To become a Master Mason you had to join a separate Master's Lodge and it was there that the distinctive ceremony and secrets were to be bestowed.

Faced with that situation and aware that even after becoming a Casual Master Mason one had still only substituted secrets it may well have seemed to the Antients that rather than have a further fight over what a Master Mason's degree ought to be able to offer it would be better to establish their own distinctive lodge practice and incorporate what was now becoming customary in their own programme. If that was the reasoning by the Antients then I wish that had been spelt out for me much earlier.

On the other hand there could have been another reason.

Could it be that when the Antients at last decided to take the truly momentous step of challenging a new kind of Grand Lodge, now known as the Premier and one that had the approval of the Government and an increasing patronage by the nobility and influential citizenry, they might well have had second thoughts?

Was it not true that there were enough immediate and pressing tasks to be tackled without seeking to question the whole concept of what was the correct and traditional three degree system and especially if they were at least able to practice the old conclusion of the third degree?

We have to realise that what most focused the attention and the concern of these 'breakaway' brethren were the many features of Premier Grand Lodge Craft working that they questioned. These included the inadequate preparation of a candidate, the incorrect arranging of the Lodge room, omitting the necessary Charges, prayers and lectures, using the wrong password for the first two degrees and the wrong word for the third after raising, neglecting the full ceremony of installing a Worshipful Master and ignoring the two saints days of St John, not to mention the general de-Christianising of the ceremonies.

When in addition to considering all those matters attention had to be given to the administering of the first influx of Lodges to their number and the task of recruiting or forming new ones it is hardly surprising that giving attention to the restoration or reintegration of an old Master's degree should not be among the primary aims of this new Grand Lodge. It is, I am sure, because of the eventual claim by Laurence Dermott that the degree of the Holy Royal Arch was *the very root, heart and marrow of Freemasonry* that in retrospect we should imagine that it would occupy the central, indeed the sole, position in the minds of this new kind of Mason, but that was not the case.

When it is further realised that Dermott was not the first Grand Secretary of this body and that there was some confusion over its management in its initial days it is even surprising that some concern over the Royal Arch should come to be seen, with hindsight, as so prominent a feature of the Antients Grand Lodge at all.

What certainly weighs with me, as probably the third and most important reason for an acceptance of the status quo as far as English Freemasonry was concerned, was the fact that it was still possible to insist in the new establishment, as had once been the tradition, that the genuine secrets of the Craft were the prerogative of the Brother who passed through the Chair of King Solomon. As has been already indicated, the Antients had to introduce afresh the whole experience of becoming a ruler in the Craft, with its attendant step of becoming a Mark Master, before anyone could be admitted, through a completed arch, into the most sacred precinct of the Temple where the full reality of the nature and presence of the True and Living God could be known and shared.

It is not a casual coincidence, as we saw at the end of the chapter on the role of the Master Mason, that his true destination as the Master and ruler of the Lodge, and his proper place of interment, was originally in the Sanctum Sanctorum itself.

There are perfectly good reasons, as present day ritual makes clear, why that earlier conclusion could not continue to be observed. What is important for us to recognise is that the Royal Arch element in English Masonry has been on a journey of development and to know from what sort of roots it has been duly transformed into what it now is. The purpose of this whole presentation is to enable the Royal Arch Companion of today to appreciate the rich components that first contributed to making the ceremony we share.

It is at this point that I want to submit an insight on what we have insisted on calling the Royal Arch but which may very well have been given a quite different title.

Could it not be that why we have for so long thought it so difficult to unravel the source of this part of our Masonry is because, as I have already hinted, it once had an existence in another form? I mean, of course, that by the end of the 17th century, at least, it had become the practice for skilled conveyors of Masonic ritual to recite a continuous account of how the true secrets of divine and human knowledge had been transmitted through the ages. I mean just such a recital as was in part revealed in the previous chapter by the usage called Heredom of Kilwinning or the Royal Order.

Indeed, we know that in the north-east of England there were, from the late 1600s, those appointed lecturers of such skill who had the variant title of Harodim or Select Masters and the instruction so shared was for those who were, or were to be, rulers in the Free and Accepted Craft. The extent of it was already such that most Brethren could not recall it, hence their uncertainty about it.

What has now to be understood is that when this whole account leading up to the disclosure of the genuine secrets of old Freemasonry was discontinued or disbanded by the growth of a 1717 London-based Freemasonry that required separate Apprentices and Master Masons, instead of only the former Fellows, and which applied the Temple of Solomon era-story to the Fellows and Masters, it left other elements of the ONCE CONTINUOUS story (my emphasis) to become a basis for other ceremonies that acquired new titles and some new forms.

It now became evident to me, whilst searching for the roots of our present Masonic degrees, that when, for example, in the 1870s, the Masons who had been entrusted with the remnants of the Ark Mariner degree finally handed it over to the new and efficient Grand Mark Lodge they still insisted that what they surrendered was 200 years old. Many at the time thought that that was boastful chatter. I have now found that 200 years to the very decade there was apparently being practised in England a form of the Noah degree.

What I am therefore saying is this.

That what was left of the complete whole tradition of Accepted Masonic teaching about the true Mason Word, spoken of in the Muses Threnodie of Perth in 1632, along with the genuine secrets of the 'red tau' or Rosy Cross, are just those that now hung unclaimed and uncared for when the Antients began to repair that loss.

It was no use seeking to relocate the Moderns form of a third degree in its old sequence. As the Irish Grand Lodge had also copied the English pattern and made it their third degree, what could the sons of that land, who mostly founded the Antients, do but follow that course.

What Laurence Dermott discovered was that in his native isle and capital they had preserved the other part of the whole story. In or near 1742 he was exalted into the Royal Arch. That name, I hasten to point out, is not the clue to its history.

It could, just as naturally, have been called the Summum Bonum or Ne Plus Ultra degree but, as has again been mentioned already, the symbol of the well-formed Arch as an appropriate picture of perfect masonry has become an idea that all can relate to. This would have been all the more natural if, as I mention elsewhere in this story, the Mark Degree ended with the replacement of the keystone to form the perfect Arch and that led sensibly to a ceremony in which a sacred temple arch in Jerusalem was the entry point to the ultimate secret. The meaning of the Arch was also explained in early Sheffield R. A. Ritual. What it is not any longer sensible to do is speak about the Holy Royal Arch degree as if, by itself, it is discoverable from its beginning as a separate entity with just one name.

It is when we begin to recast our thinking so as to accept the Royal Arch as the reintegrated part of an earlier whole that we begin to restate our answers to two questions that have for long exercised Freemasons.

One is, is the Royal Arch the completion of the present Master Mason's degree? The second is, do we know who devised this part of Freemasonry and why? The proper answer to the first question has to be that it enables the third degree to become part of its original whole and explains the Solomonic portion of Freemasonry within its triple setting of the Mosaic Tabernacle and the Second Temple.

As far as the second question goes, we do not know who was the initial creator but originally those parts were also embraced within the even wider revelation of Adam's fall and his redemption by the second Adam – Christ – a Christian presentation that was, as we shall see, constantly retained in some 18th century Chapter rituals.

Indeed, it was because the Moderns had reordered significant parts of the ritual of the three degrees without their more specifically Christian features that the Antients took the steps they did.

It was to restore for Freemasons the true dimension of the Temple, the whole disclosure of the Word and Name of the Divine, and the admission of a

Companion, first into the select body of the Sanhedrin and finally, through the Chapter chairs, into the very High Priesthood itself.

It is as that fuller picture of what Accepted Craft Freemasonry was in fact really all about was now revived that to view the Master Mason degree, however it may seem, as a completion could be no longer true.

It was not only that the Antients stood for this 'something more'. It was they who alone preserved this older tradition for our benefit and enhanced it during the rest of the 18th century. It is in this context that we can properly appreciate what Laurence Dermott wrote on how to further the popularity and membership of the Royal Arch:

1. *By declaring it to be an integral part of pure, ancient Masonry that had come down from time immemorial, thereby giving it an air of both authority and antiquity.*
2. *By permitting it to be worked in their Craft lodges by virtue of their Craft warrants.*
3. *By making it not a separate form of Freemasonry but the fourth degree in the Craft.*
4. *By emphasising its value and its importance because it seeks to introduce us to the ultimate essentials of our Order.*

In regard to that second point it needs to be noted that the *'Royal Arch was not SPECIFIED in the lodge charter, but was regarded as such a completely integral part of the Masonic scheme as not to need mention. It was just taken for granted. And to that statement must be added a further one: under their ordinary charters or warrants, the Antients, the Irish and many of the Scottish Lodges ... believed they had the right to confer any and every Masonic degree they pleased.'* (B.E. Jones op. cit. p.58)

Is it any wonder that so many degrees were spread by the Army lodges warranted by these bodies?

The Antients had a parallel publication to the Moderns' Constitutions. It was called 'Ahiman Rezon' (to be pronounced as 'aheeman retsown') or 'A Secretary's Companion', because it contained all the decrees of their Grand Lodge and hence much advice about procedure for the Scribe Ezra of a Chapter. In the 1807 edition we have these comments:

> *'This degree is certainly more august, sublime and important than those which precede it, and is the summit and perfection of Antient Masonry. It impresses on our minds a more firm belief (note: not an initial awareness) of the existence of a Supreme Deity, without beginning of days or end of years and justly reminds us of the respect and veneration due to that Holy Name.'*
> (p. 106)

As Bro Batham adds:

> *'The Freemasons of those days were, in the main, of a deeply religious kind and it was natural for them to resent the de-Christianisation of the ritual ...'*

Dermott's promotion of this essentially spiritual aspect of the Craft, as he saw it, must have contributed to the rapid growth of the Antients' membership. However, the insistence on being an Installed Master for admission, whilst marking the Arch's importance and selectivity, began to be a disadvantage and so gave rise to a new development in Antients' Lodges.

It was called the 'Passing the Chair degree'.

I quote from Companion Batham again:

> 'A way to circumvent the regulation was soon found. Who was responsible is unknown but presumably it was some enthusiastic brother or group of brethren in one of their Lodges, for it was certainly not introduced by Grand Lodge. The solution was the creation of a new ceremony, the 'Passing the Chair' degree. This was an abbreviated installation ceremony in which, surprising as it may now seem, a Master Mason was given the secrets of an Installed Master and allowed to occupy the chair of his lodge for a few minutes and thus become what was known as a virtual Past Master. From a Craft point of view he remained a Master Mason, was not allowed to view the Inner Working and, if he subsequently became Master-elect, had to go through the full Installation ceremony. Nevertheless, it qualified him for admission to the Royal Arch.' (op. cit. p.91)

As Deputy Grand Master, Dermott *expatiated for a long time on the scandalous method pursued by most of the Lodges (on St. John's days) in passing a Number of Brethren through the chair on purpose to obtain the sacred Mystery's of the ROYAL ARCH and therefore moved for a Regulation to be made in order to Suppress them for the future*'. (Grand Lodge meeting, December 1771, Dermott's emphasis)

What is certain is that the practice was not, and could not be, suppressed as we shall see later in this book. It is noteworthy that the Antients registered Exaltees admitted by this method but did not include them in official returns. What is clear is that enthusiasm for the Holy Royal Arch remained unabated and not only were the Antients now described as the 'Grand Lodge of the Four Degrees' but many Moderns Masons were now eager to share in this development.

Such then was the fashion in which this traditional and essential element of English Freemasonry was restored to use. That it should have originated in an atmosphere of ill-feeling or antipathy is regrettable but looking back on the events of the mid-century one can only be glad that for whatever reasons this aspect of our whole Craft was once more regained.

Certainly that was the opinion of a certain offspring of George II. The effect of his experience and influence is what will occupy us next.

The First Grand Chapter

'The first-known English minute recording the raising of a Brother to the R(oyal) A(rch) is, perhaps unexpectedly, of a 'MODERNS' lodge at Bristol, in 1758, but it would be wrong to rush to the conclusion from this isolated evidence that the 'Moderns' worked the Royal Arch earlier than the Antients.'
(B.E. Jones. op. cit. p. 50. His emphasis)

What we are also told is that from this first instance on Sunday, August 13th 1758, until May 6, 1759, seven Royal Arch meetings were held and 13 brethren 'raised' quite shortly after becoming just Master Masons.

Already, though in a private letter, the celebrated Thomas Dunckerley had reported that he was made a Royal Arch Mason in his Moderns lodge at Portsmouth in 1754, so the idea that all Moderns Masons adopted the stance which we examined in a previous chapter is certainly not the case.

Indeed, by 1766 there were so many Moderns Royal Arch members that they were now able to make their voice heard and request that no less a person than Cadwallader, Lord Blayney, should accept the post of Most Excellent Grand Master of Royal Arch Masonry.

This distinguished brother had been Grand Master of the Moderns Grand Lodge from 1764 to 1766 and was to be Grand Master of Ireland in 1768. It is revealing that he was a close friend of Thomas Dunckerley, appointed him to high office and shared with that brother a strong leaning towards, and sympathy for, Antients working.

It has to be remarked that foremost as his Lordship was in seeking to promote the Royal Arch he was not the first Grand Master to take this step for the later Earl of Lanesborough had already set the pattern as a previous Grand Master of Ireland. For men who were the heads of institutions that firmly stressed a 'three degrees only' tradition their practice speaks volumes.

Accordingly in 1766, and enough has now been said over the years to show that it was 1766 and not 1767, a Charter of Compact was formally instituted and signed by 30 persons with some of their seals. It bears the Royal coat of arms and those of the Premier Grand Lodge and Lord Blayney, and nine triangles that are meant to represent the three Principals, three Sojourners, Scribe E., Scribe N. and the Altar. There are words at the head of the Charter that are commonly found on all the early Grand Chapter documents – The Most Enlightened East – while the letters I.N. in a central triangle are interpreted by some as 'Ineffable Name' but which, considering the ethos of that period, could represent 'Iesus Nazarenus' or Jesus of Nazareth.

If they do mean the latter then it confirms my own conviction that the de-Christianisation of English Masonry only really took place at and after the 1813

Union. What Anderson, a good son of Presbyterianism, did was to replace denominationalism with that basic Christian faith common to men.

What he certainly could not have been at that date was a multi-faith protagonist.

The declared purpose of the new Grand Chapter was now plain to see in the words that were used. It was to *'carry on, improve and promote the said benevolent and useful Work'*.

That suggests that what we call the Royal Arch had already proved itself to be of benefit to Freemasonry. It was to *'admit, pass and exalt in due form and according to the Rites and Ceremonies Time Immemorial used and approved, in and by that most Exalted and sacred Degree'*.

Here, we are pointed to more than a simple ceremony of 'exaltation' for there are steps through which a candidate should be admitted and passed.

To what that refers we must return below and in the next chapter dealing with the developing ritual and legends. We are certainly reassured that here is no new-fangled 30 years old practice but rites and ceremonies that can claim *'Time Immemorial use'* status. Could it actually be pre-1700?

Coming from the stable of those who had for so long claimed that they and they alone represented 'old Masonry' this is a surprising declaration. When there are added the words *'most Exalted and sacred'* we would seem to be hinting at the divine throne, high and lifted up, as Isaiah described it, and situated in the Holy of Holies.

This wording is both enlightening and somewhat overwhelming.

It is in the tail of this document that there was a potential sting. The subjects of this new endeavour were *'all such experienced & discreet Master Masons as they shall find worthy'*. This seemed to set the Grand Chapter on another collision course with the Antients who had been so adamant that only installed Masters could become Royal Arch Masons that a separate device to ensure that had been devised. Yet elsewhere in the Charter of Compact there is an eighth clause stating that

> *'none calling themselves Royal Arch Masons shall be deemed any other than Masters in operative Masonry'.*

At this point a comment by Bro B.E. Jones is timely.

> *'This assumption appears to echo the claim to superior status made in earlier years by the SCOTCH MASONS ... and its presence in the Charter, besides strengthening any supposition that the earlier rite was related to the later one, may help us to arrive at an answer to a difficult question: how came it about the new Grand Chapter with no experience of ESOTERIC INSTALLATION, was so soon to insist on a Past Master qualification in its Candidates? Is the answer, or some part of it, that, regarding itself as an association of MASTERS,*

it eagerly took a leaf from its opponent's book to ensure that only (Past) Masters entered into its membership? ... the truth may well be somewhere (here).' (op. cit. p. 76. Author's emphases)

At the risk of repetition may I point out that here is the justification for having spent so much time and space in this presentation on the unravelling of the status and meaning of the term 'Master Mason' at different periods. At last the Premier Grand Lodge was having to resolve this important issue.

What is a fact is that in 1778, and I use Bro Batham's words, *'for reasons that cannot be readily understood'*, the Grand Chapter ruled that candidates for this degree were acceptable only if they had

> *'been regularly apprenticed and presided as Masters, to be justly entitled to, and have received the Past Masters' token and pass word'.*

This is an even more remarkable declaration because it speaks of a *'regular apprenticeship and presiding'* as a Master and that conjures up a formal presentation to and instruction in that office. It also speaks of receiving the *'token and pass word'* and this indicates that the Moderns were even willing to accept the validity of the extended Inner Working and Passing the Chair ceremony.

What is certain is that as early as the next year a Moderns Lodge in Bolton, Lancashire, was working the Passing the Chair ceremony.

Following the establishment of the first Grand Chapter there was a notable increase and development in both systems, the Moderns and the Antients.

The Grand Chapter began issuing charters to Lodges authorising them to work the Royal Arch and by 1800 that body had issued 116 such permissions. This charter had to be attached to the Lodge warrant thus ensuring a link between any Chapter and a Lodge. It is true that there was an evident division between the Lodge and Chapter with each having separate minute books and days of meeting. What is now steadily evident is that the terms Chapter and Companion are used but the substitution of 'exaltation' for 'raising' came more slowly.

An indication of the more tentative view of the Royal Arch that still persisted amongst the Moderns is reflected in a 1774 letter from the Grand Secretary to a foreign correspondent.

James Heseltine wrote:

> *'It is true that many of the Fraternity belong to a degree in Masonry which is said to be higher than the other, and is called the Royal Arch. I have the honour to belong to this degree. ... but it is not acknowledged in Grand Lodge, and all its emblems and jewels are forbidden to be worn there ... you will see that the Royal Arch is a private and distinct society.'* (Jones op. cit. p.80)

A year later he was telling another correspondent that *'the explanations of Freemasonry (in the Royal Arch) are very pleasing and instructive'* and in addition to its ceremonial benefits it seems that the Grand Chapter had a strong social side.

Its annual festival was followed by a ball and supper to which Master Masons and their ladies were also invited. In 1782 there were 400 ladies and gentlemen present. Yet even as there was this endeavour to make membership of the Royal Arch pleasurable as well as worthwhile we note that in the Chapter of Emulation there was a proposal that Companions should no longer support Grand Chapter. Their appeal to other Chapters was not endorsed and in due course Emulation Chapter No. 16 was erased.

Whilst the Moderns were thus engaged in at last promoting this further step in Masonry the Antients were bound to reconsider their attitude to what was now a 'Fourth Degree'.

Since their view had always been, and rightly, that this part of 'pure ancient Masonry had come down from time immemorial' so they were now unwilling to separate it from the body that regulated their whole Masonic practice, the Grand Lodge.

In reaction to the promptings of certain Antients Masons who felt that there should be a separate body overlooking the Royal Arch a subordinate committee of the Grand Lodge was appointed and, just to complicate matters, it was entitled, The Grand Chapter.

Bro Batham has a clear judgement on this move:

> *'This was no more than a token gesture as it never had a separate existence and apparently did not keep minutes of its proceedings, as none have survived. It had no officers of its own, as all fees collected were paid over to Grand Lodge. It had no powers other than those delegated to it and its proceedings were reported to Grand Lodge and all its decisions were subject to ratification. This meant that Grand Lodge had the power to overrule them and this applied even to their bylaws. In other words, control of the Royal Arch degree remained very firmly in the hands of Grand Lodge.'* (Collected Papers p.94)

Eventually, in the light of several irregular makings of Royal Arch Masons, *'Nine Excellent Master Masons'* were set up to assist the Grand Officers and their task was to examine all those who were to perform Royal Arch ceremonies.

I find their title intriguing since these were obviously much more skilled and experienced brethren than those usually carrying this title.

Were they the Antients' form of Harodim, the Past Masters who could guide and instruct the newer Lodge Masters in the detail and meaning of such ceremonies as they would now have to conduct? It is revealing that nine years later they were consulted on the future correct type of Royal Arch clothing.

What has to be said at this juncture is that the steps taken by both the Antients and the Moderns in reassessing their modes of controlling the admission to, and conferring of, the Holy Royal Arch degree not only increased the numbers of those being Exalted but raised the awareness of what the Royal Arch degree was and where it belonged in the whole panoply of the Craft.

That these efforts had a marked effect on what would happen when Union was considered is certain. The results thereafter make up their own story but before we can usefully consider that period we need to take a much more detailed look at what exactly was the Holy Royal Arch of Jerusalem degree as the 18th century took its latter course.

How did the Royal Arch Legends and Ritual develop?

What we will be considering here is that part of the developing story that attended and then followed the emergence of what was now called the Royal Arch, along with the ideas and symbolic references which led to what we call its ceremonies.

What may surprise you, as it once did me, is the fact that even today we are dependent on more than one legend or story for conducting this part of our Masonry. We are not talking here, as many still seem to imagine, about one simple tale. A few moments reflection on present practice will help to underline this point.

What is it that a candidate is being expected to 'take in' at his Exaltation, or at meetings after our own admission? Just what is it that we later have time to think about as having happened to us on that occasion?

On coming to light in the Chapter we find ourselves in an environment totally different to that of our Craft Lodges, surrounded by ensigns of some kind bearing the symbols of the 12 Hebrew tribes.

We stand before an arch, or the place where arch stones were removed, and yet the impression is of being in some kind of tunnel or vault. Various implements lie scattered before us with an array of six lights around, or beyond, a white pillar which is like two cubic stones set on top of one other.

The pillar is covered with a cloth and alongside it, at the far end of the ensigns, are probably two Companions wearing white garments or surplices. Beyond them are three figures in robes of red, purple and blue holding three rods or sceptres formed in the shape of an equilateral triangle with, behind them, five larger banners showing four creatures and a strange device, whilst all around are other Companions who are either grasping the staves of the ensigns or holding their own separate plain white rods with which they create a kind of pointed roof for the vault.

Where did the need for all these things come from?

Even when we have discovered the legendary or even historical backgrounds to all this, what about the Sojourners, the implements they are given, their use of cords, the story that one of them tells, and the items that are handed over at the investiture?

Oh yes, and there will already have been needed an explanation of what lies behind the catechism that is still exchanged between the MEZ and the Principal Sojourner either in the Chapter or at the festive board later?

As soon as we list just the items with which we are so familiar today the variety of background can be seen to be much more complex than might at first appear.

Nor, of course, have we yet included the contents of the three appointed lectures or the Installation ceremonies for the three Principals.

About these I shall say something later.

We are not, I repeat, inheritors of a single, simple story as we might at first be led to believe. Our ceremony nowadays is indeed much simpler than it used to be but it is still one that has preserved traces of several influences that affected the Royal Arch tradition for a century and more. It is in an attempt to uncover those many backgrounds that I now turn.

Because what we now call the Holy Royal Arch was at its inception part and parcel of Guild Craft Freemasonry, two features have to be kept in mind. The first feature has to be the traditional history that we find in the 16th and 17th century Old Charges, to which I have earlier referred. What were the sources that combined to provide the backcloth to what was to be the fresh form of the old, or Geometrical, Master Mason degree?

One answer, as I have sought to provide in my book, *Let me tell you more,* is the then acknowledged historical writing of the monks and especially the work of Sir Ranulph Higden of St Werburgha's Abbey, Chester. His work, *The Polychronicon,* was given the royal approval and is specifically mentioned in the Cooke Ms. What seems undoubted is that with the arrival of the Accepted Freemasons in the Masons Guild Lodges there comes a steady stream of traditional Christian teaching. Could it also be that some of the now homeless monks and priests also joined this body and brought their special knowledge and traditions?

There was yet another strand of influence, the more so as the 17th century progressed, and that was the introduction of Hebraic ideas through the presence, not only of an increasing Jewish population's input with the support of the Protector, Oliver Cromwell, but of the Christian Cabbalistic scholarship which began in the reign of the Tudors and was now becoming more widely known in the better educated section of the public.

Eighty years ago there appeared on the Masonic scene an author named the Revd Frederick Castells. His six books are almost entirely devoted to a study of the early development of the Holy Royal Arch and by the time his last book, *The Genuine Secrets in Freemasonry,* was published he was known as one holding extremely decided views about the early nature of this Order.

Those views could be summed up by saying that the Holy Royal Arch was, as Dermott claimed, the very *'root, heart and marrow'* of Freemasonry, but for Castells it was also a Jewish institution and it was heavily dependent upon Cabbalism for much of its content as a form of teaching.

As examples of his claim I select first the following passage found by the historian, Bro Gould, in an *'essay bound up with, and forming part of, the BOOK OF CONSTITUTIONS of 1738',* which says:

> *'The Cabbalists, another Sect, dealt in hidden and mysterious Ceremonies. The Jews had a great Regard for this Science, and thought that they made uncommon discoveries by means of it. They divided their knowledge into SPECULATIVE and OPERATIVE. David and Solomon, they say, were*

exquisitely skilled in it; and nobody first presumed to commit it to WRITING: but … the perfection of their skill consisted in what the Dissector calls the LETTERING OF IT, by ordering the letters of the Word in a particular manner.' (op. cit. pp. 19f)

The Dissector referred to was Samuel Prichard, who in 1730 had published his exposure, *Masonry Dissected.*

Again Castells writes:

'It is from the Cabbalists that the Old Freemasons received the conception of King Solomon's Temple as the source and centre of the Genuine Secrets. Hence the description of our predecessors as Our Holy Ancestors, the atoning priests.' (op. cit. p. 71)

There is no doubt that in his day Bro Castells was eventually regarded as extremist in his views and was accordingly shunned by other students of the Royal Arch.

To those, however, who take the trouble to read his works and weigh his arguments, where based on evidence, there has to come the realisation that much that seems difficult, if not impossible, to unravel, or is otherwise mysterious, begins at last to make sense and to form a coherent pattern.

This is not to concur in the view that Cabbalism is, or is the only, source of Chapter legend and practice. What has to be conceded is that if we are to discover the answers to many Royal Arch issues then this form of knowledge, whether it be Rabbinic, or Christian, Cabbalism, has to be considered as a contributing factor.

Of course there will be those Freemasons who are wary of what might appear to be the occult intimations that the term 'Cabbala' evokes. To such brethren one has to reply that if this sort of knowledge was in part what our predecessors employed in the developing of Chapter ritual and practice then that is a fact that we may regret but have to accept.

What has also to be said is that whereas there is no doubt about some Cabbalistic influence in matters of numerology, symbolatry and commentary, it is all encompassed by what in the 18th century was a Christian context. Jews could begin to appreciate the Craft and Royal Arch because it had an Hebraic thread, or threads, but as the ritual which follows will reveal there could at that stage be little question as to what was the ultimate goal of the Order. It wasw designed to be a recital of the full Christian revelation.

The second feature to which I referred above is what I call a 'discovery element'. This is hardly surprising because the main component of a Masonic ceremony is taking the right steps, or grades, to uncover the secret, or secrets, of that degree. Yet whilst the path of 'discovery', in what were called the three probationary degrees, is a spoken word, along with a grip or token, the discovery which early began to distinguish the Royal Arch was that of an object that only one who was a true Master Mason or Grand Master could possess.

Before we come to what such items might have been, and why, there was another tradition that was closely associated with that feature. This element was linked, as several early exposures of ritual show, with 'the rule of three'.

That idea appears in the Graham Manuscript and in the work by Prichard already referred to where he uses the then contemporary words *'If you would a Master Mason be then you must learn the rule of three'.*

This, with other indications in those, and parallel, rituals, shows that what was later to be called 'the Royal Arch step' was already in place as the Summum Bonum or culmination of Masonry.

Leading up to the later idea of a 'supreme degree' were stories that linked this progress with several groups of three persons. That seems very likely to have been due to Rabbinic influence.

Pre-eminently at this time, of course, there was the overriding idea of the Trinity, the still widely held belief that behind the whole creative activity of the Deity there were three 'personae' or aspects – Father, Son and Holy Spirit – and as this style of Godhead was that which comprised the G.A.O. T.U., the Grand Geometrician and the Most High, so the form of rule at the culmination of Freemasonry was thought of as a rule by 'three as one'.

This, of course, was much more evident in my own early days in this Order when, as part of the presentation of the Mystical Lecture we used the terms, 'Father Lord, Word Lord and Spirit Lord'.

Nor was this the only representation of 'the rule of three'.

In some old Lodge rooms you can still see a large pre-Union Tracing Board with a classical-style domed pavilion, upon, and under, the roof of which there stand three pairs of three characters.

These are Moses, Aholiab and Bezaleel; Solomon, Hiram of Tyre and Hiram Abi; Zerubbabel, Haggai and Joshua, representing the three periods of the sacred Old Testament story.

Yet even this was not the only concept which lay behind the rule of three which is now such a trademark of the Royal Arch and of the derivative degrees known as Royal and Select which were once part of the developed Royal Arch lectures.

What was as old, operatively, was the legend of Pythagoras discovering the perfect dimensions that produced a right-angled triangle, declaring that it was in the proportion of 3:4:5. It was that which was long regarded as the essential secret, which only a Master Mason who had been admitted to the central building secret, expressed in Freemasonry as 'those through the Chair', could obtain.

Hence the requirement that only those who had so 'passed the Chair' could be Royal Arch Masons and hence the adoption of the special jewel for those who were not just Immediate Past Masters but for all Past Masters.

As will no doubt have become clear to the reader only Installed Masters were eventually granted admission to the Royal Arch. By the latter half of the 18th century, however, it was becoming obvious that the strict application of this rule was delaying entry to what the Antients truly believed was THE essential part of Masonry.

Passing the Chair

There was thus introduced a device which was designed to enable a Third Degree Mason who had NOT been, or been elected to be, the ruler of a Lodge to have the status that would permit him to be a candidate for the Chapter.

The device was called Passing the Chair.

It was first adopted by the Antients, since they so strongly emphasised the Installing ceremony as a Time-Immemorial practice, but it was then taken up by some Moderns' lodges as they also restricted entry to the Royal Arch to Installed Masters.

On such an occasion it was stressed that this was an interim ceremony and did not confer the usual privileges associated with being the ruler of a Lodge. One development that is worth noting, as the century progressed, is that the ceremony took place in a Chapter rather than a Lodge.

There are, of course, several examples of what took place at such a Passing but that recorded in the one-time notebook of an Alexander Dalziel of Newcastle-on-Tyne, but from 1949 in the possession of a Bruce Oliver of Barnstaple, gives us a clear impression. This was a usage from 1790 onwards.

Members of a Chapter opened a Lodge in the Past Master degree prior to the Exaltation and declared it as dedicated to *the noble prince Adoniram*.

The usual but full Installation opening was used and the customary obligation. The candidate was then given a distinguishing mark that will interest both Mark and Ark Mariner Masons, namely AS, that represented Adoniram and the Sidonians, who were noted as the perfecters of the Porphyry.

The signs then given were those used in what we now call the extended working, laying most emphasis on the plumbline. He was invested with the Master's jewel, exhorted to act in his new guise with discretion and then politely requested to forsake the Chair, whereupon his Master's jewel was replaced with that of a Past Master.

He was then usually invited to regale his installing brethren with refreshment. It has to be recorded that by the 1820s some Lodges had become so unaware of the 'ancient usage' at Installation that this ceremony was adopted in its place.

The Items of Recognition

Reverting to the actual items that have been used and bestowed in the development of this Order we see that they all relate to the above connections.

They were a rod or rule, a jewel or stone and a sacred document. One of these, the ROD, combined with the rods of the other Grand Masters, not only verified the status of the holder as a recognised ruler but assisted in retaining the 'secret' which three rulers *'or three such as we'* alone possessed and which, if one of them was temporarily removed, impaired the full secret being known or acted upon.

Delving into the symbolic background of the ROD brings some interesting things to light. The Deity himself is shown in medieval pictures and windows wielding a rod at the Last Judgement when he directs the blessed to Heaven and the evil to Hell.

It is therefore no surprise to see that in many old Bibles the Patriarchs – Enoch, Noah, Abraham, Moses, Aaron and Samuel – are all fitted out with rods.

It was for this reason that amongst the medieval workmen only the Master Mason was allowed to possess and wield such an item. If you have ever wondered, therefore, where the idea comes from of presenting our Exaltees with a rod or staff when they are invested you may now be somewhat clearer. Possession of a rod symbolised their being real Master Masons.

Moreover, the three Principals have in fact three rods which have been transformed into sceptres as a result of the changeover from Enoch, Noah and Shem to the princely Moses, Solomon, Hiram of Tyre and Zerubbabel, not to mention, for Old York and Irish Masons, King Josiah.

Following the Pythagorean legend of the three varied 'rules' you may care to know that in York and Ireland in the 17th and early 18th centuries the Right Worshipful Master and Wardens of a Lodge, in which the earliest form of what would later be called the Royal Arch was practised, each held respectively a rod of 30", 24" and 18".

When an Exaltee now sees the three Principals with their rods in a triangular form he is witnessing the eventual merger of at least three legendary sources – the Trinitarian, Hermetic and operative.

The discovery of a jewel that determined who was a true MM was, as the reader may recall, mentioned earlier as part of the De Bouillon degree practised in the 1730s. That was, by any standards, a remarkable revelation.

It showed how, by an early date in London, the completion of the Temple of Solomon, the discovery of an Arch and the Ark of the Covenant, belief in the Trinity or a tripartite rule, the use of holy words and a discovery of special objects were already incorporated into the completing degree of the Craft.

What is interesting is that the London Premier Grand Lodge could not then accept this form of a true Master Mason degree and both this Lodge, and any like it, were by 1753 formally excluded from that Grand Lodge's recognised list.

The reasons behind this decision seem understandable in the circumstances. Ordinary Master Masons had been refused admission by the De Bouillon Lodges and the Premier Grand Lodge could clearly not endorse the working of such Lodges without admitting that their own third degree was incomplete.

The Interment Theme

The fact that the growing Royal Arch story was, as the evedence indicates, connected with a discovery in or near a symbolic grave, it is not surprising that, as a separate step was required that would be called 'the Royal Arch', it was also related to an underground chamber below the Temple.

The legends that gave rise to this idea were, first, a tradition that Hiram Abi had, at the request of Solomon, created a meeting place for the three Grand Masters beneath the Holy of Holies, the innermost sanctuary called the 'debir'.

In the earliest Sheffield ritual we read these words by the Sojourner:

'These 7 pair (of) Pillars supported a roof under which K(ing) S(olomon) had a secret passage from the centre of the Temple to this Arch where he used to go and adore the (Most High:) this roof was destroyed when the Temple was (demolished) but the Arch remained sound till we broke in and found . . .'

Another tradition states that this was also meant to be the possible hiding place for the Ark of the Covenant. There was still another tradition that when the Grand Master Architect was finally buried he was laid in this underground spot where the secret that he died to protect was not only always known but regularly shared.

For anyone unfamiliar with this latter idea may I quote from Prichard's exposure of the ritual in 1730:

'What was done with the body of our very worthy Master?'
'Solomon, to reward his zeal and talents, had him buried in the Sanctum Sanctorum.'

At first sight this may seem contrary to what was said about burial BENEATH the Sanctum Sanctorum but three things have to be remembered. Prichard is probably emphasizing the ultimate destination of a Master Mason which we have already seen was the holy of Holies. Secondly, though this is legend yet we have to remember that the Sanctum Sanctorum was not yet consecrated by King Solomon and the rules about burial there need not apply. Thirdly, however, Hiram Abi is said to have been BURIED and therefore we may conclude that he was lowered below the site. This would fit prefectly with a vault beneath. The usual conclusion of most writers on this topic is that he was buried NEAR the Holy of Holies but how near is not known.

In another ritual soon after we also read this:

'What did he have placed upon the Tomb?'
A golden medallion in the shape of a triangle, on which was engraved JHVH, the former word of a Master, which is the name of God in Hebrew.'

That triangle and the letters are STILL placed on the coffin in a presentation of the third degree in Holland and parts of France, but is never explained in that degree. Hence, at least, arose the idea of a subterranean crypt or vault, which would seem to conflict with the other legend about discovering the keystone of an arch.

The Arch Concept

The arch has already been mentioned in terms of the item that completed the work of the First Temple.

Even as this book was being written its author had a singular experience. He attended a demonstration Festival of the Mark degrees in the Midlands and saw something that he had not witnessed here before.

When the Worshipful Master had commended the Mason on not only carving *'the most important stone in the building'* but also finding it again intact after being wrongly discarded, the Keystone was lifted from in front of the Master Overseer's pedestal and, being held aloft and with respect, was brought to the frame in front of the Worshipful Master and set in its proper place to complete an arch.

This ceremonial act I had never before seen in England, though I was made a candidate in the Most Excellent Master degree in Toronto where the same procedure has become a separate ceremony. It was once known as the 'Arch Degree'.

It is, of course, a natural and essential link connecting the Mark and the Royal Arch.

Yet this was not the only legend that referred to such an item.

Into 17th century thinking there had been introduced the story of the arches of Enoch that led to a secret place of knowledge. The echo of this story is still with us in the Sojourner's account of a series of exquisite pillars that supported an arched passageway leading to the vault with its domed roof.

The Holy Royal Arch ritual of 1760 is the earliest complete one we have and this clearly illustrates this combination. The ritual appears in a set of eight grades preserved in an ornate French Ms.

This informs us of an underground chamber which is supported by nine arches with nine steps by which to descend into it. It is also opened with nine knocks and the reader will be aware that earlier we saw one example of why nine was an appropriate number in this degree. (See p.50)

There is now an explanation of a tracing board on which the sun is shown to be the true light that led the nine brethren (sic) to discover the great secret. The board also depicts nine arches, the vault of an underground chamber and the nine steps. There is also a stone, with a ring, closing the chamber (that should interest Irish and Scottish Companions), a torch which has been extinguished by the sun's brilliance and, again, a triangular plate of gold bearing the Sacred Name.

The Ms. refers, in explanation of a sign, to the action of *'a priest as he says Mass'* when repeating *'Dominus vobiscum'* (The Lord be with you) and extending his hands over the elements, a sign formerly given to all Royal Arch Masons.

The Word, like all the rest in cypher, is IA BUL UM and is the only word to be shared by three.

More will be said about this later.

The password is Iehovah and I AM THAT I AM. This latter will be recognised as the name of the Deity given to Moses in the Sinai desert.

This working already demonstrates the amalgamation of a Rabbinic legend about the underground chamber and an Enoch tradition of the arches.

In a later 1765 version of this working we might note the following variations. On striking with his pick, one of the Sojourners finds the stone with a ring at its centre and using ropes they remove this slab and find the chamber beneath. The discoverer of the stone is GIBILLUM and he agrees to descend but is twice withdrawn when he is seized with panic at arches three and six. He descends once more with the torch and reaches the ninth arch.

A piece of the wall facing him crumbles and he sees a triangular stone covering the sacred word.

In a state of awe he stretches out his hands as SOLOMON did when he commissioned them for this work. He then fell on his knees with one hand behind his back and the other shading his eyes. Then he retreated, pulled on his cord and was lifted out, to do which the other Sojourners used the following grip: to extend the hands as if ready to lift another out of a hole.

Finally, all three Sojourners descended into the chamber and at the ninth arch lifted the stone and found the sacred word.

The whole influence of Noah and his family, not to mention his ARK, was present in some of the earliest catechisms that we possess. The symbolism of the Rainbow as the first sacred Arch, signifying God's care for the mankind he created, and the revealing of his purpose for his people, was yet another story giving support to the adoption of the Arch as the culmination of Masonic truth.

The Deptford, Dovre and Dalziel Rituals

The mention of Noah leads us naturally into the next stage of Royal Arch ritual development. In 1880 an old box in the vaults of St Paul's Church, Deptford, was found to contain two volumes written in cypher.

They were a Royal Arch ritual and parts of the ceremony of making a Geometrical or Geomatic Mason from 1769. The combination of the two underlines the main theme of my earlier thesis, that there was a distinction between the casual Master Mason that emerged after 1726 and a much older form of that grade.

In the obligation of this Chapter of Most Excellent Master Masons there is an additional penalty that will not be unfamiliar to some Past Masters today, that, no less, of *my tongue cleaving to the roof of my mouth and remaining dumb for a season*.

Later, the candidate will hear a prayer that concludes:

'Grant, O Lord, that while we are expounding this Christian lecture we may obtain a right view of... the Sacred Mysteries of the holy gospel of Jesus Christ,

*and grant, O Lord that we may all be united... in keeping the secrets of this our
Most Excellent Order, sacred and unviolated...for the sake of Jesus Christ our
Lord and Saviour.'*

Whilst it is obviously impossible to reproduce the whole of this 'Most Sublime
Order' there are a few extracts that need further exposure at this stage of English
Masonry so as to enable us to savour this form, and also other later forms of
Chapter working that disappeared in the 19th century.

Thus, in the opening, the Master asks:

'Where was this Order first established?'
*'On the high and lofty top of Mount Moriah, the low and humble Vale of
Jehosaphat, far from the crowing of a cock, barking of a dog, noise of a hammer
or any tool of metal that might disturb the silence and the harmony...'*

The high and low points here mentioned were to enable the Janitor to see that all
who approach are qualified; the crowing cock was to remind us not to need a
monitor like St Peter who might betray his Master; the angry dog was to warn us
of those who might be unwanted members; and the mention of tools recalled
Exodus chap. 29 where Moses was told not to use such items lest God's holy altar
be polluted.

What then comes as a surprise, after recalling the raising of Hiram with the
F.P.O.F., is the beginning of most of the rest of the ritual which is in almost
identical terms as that of the Heredom of Kilwinning to which I referred earlier.

It is true that the Royal Order has 14 sections whereas this Deptford ritual has
only nine but both of them end on the same identical note:

'How did you receive these glad and welcome tidings?'
*'With an ecstasy of Joy, saying, Glory to God on high, Peace on earth, and good
will towards men.'* (Now perhaps we see where this passage used today
originates.)
'What was the righteous brother's name?'
'Joseph.'
'What was the name of his holy spouse?'
'Mary.'
'What was the ever Blessed Word?'
'Jesus.'
*'Then may the ever blessed Spirit of the Blessed Jesus be ever with us and remain
with us always.'*

Recognising this as the core of the ceremony it only remains to mention the
outline of the rest.

Having first ascertained that the candidate was of fair reputation, had some
learning and was divested of bigotry, was a proven philanthropist and of 23 or

more years, he is then slipshod, knees bared, a cord placed around his waist and he is hoodwinked.

The candidate is invited to undertake a short vigil of recollection, receive a short exhortation from a Scribe or Past Master, and after giving the Installed Master password learns the steps.

After various questions about his status he prays as the Third Principal lays his hands on the candidate's head. He is then asked to draw out two keystones (sic) *'Which will let you see light'* and then there are a set of readings from the books of Proverbs, Psalms, Ezra, Exodus and the Epistle of Peter.

He is then obligated, brought to light and seated so as to enable him to hear the former catechisms.

In 1959, Bro Norman Hackney wrote a paper on a French 'Dovre' ritual used in the Chapter of that name from 1784, and compared it with the later Deptford working in Hope Chapter No. 49, dating from 1787.

His findings were significant because not only did they reveal the variations between these two contemporary bodies but they also showed how there had been marked developments in the Deptford working.

This was possible because in the documents relating to Hope Chapter and a Prudence Chapter at Ipswich, there were two sets of workings, one of them being of 'a considerably earlier date' which, in the case of Deptford, would fit well with the working described above.

The chief differences between the Dovre (Do) and the Deptford (De) rituals in the 1780s are that:

1. In (Do) the candidate is instructed in the grips and signs before he is seated, viz.before the Sojourners enact their discovery drama. In (De) they are given by the Sojourners during their cross-examination by the MEZ. We should note that the former long catechism of (De) has been partially replaced by this more dramatic enactment.

2. In (Do) the candidate is obligated on John's Gospel ch. 1, v. 1 whereas in (De) it is *"on either the Old or New Testament, as may be deemed more obligatory from the former principles of the initiate"*. The strictly Christian stance of the latter has clearly changed.

3. In (Do) there are only three lecture sections whilst in (De) the nine sections have been reduced to five. What is more the first three at (De) are similar to those in (Do) and the others are in a rudimentary form somewhat like what would be introduced after 1835.

4. In (Do) the three Principals demonstrate the method of sharing the Word by standing round the altar with their right hand resting upon it; in (De) there is no mention of any such instruction. This seems to suggest that the early methods of word sharing were much simpler than today.

5. In (Do) there is a brief suggestion of a formal closing ceremony: a hymn and prayer with all the members kneeling. The Companions then depart and the Principals alone close the Chapter as they did the Opening. In English Chapters there does not seem to be any such closing. It needs to be added that in all these rituals the Scripture readings are all from the New Testament and the words on the scroll that is found are those from John's Gospel, ch. 1.

Mention must here be made of a most distinctive ritual of the mid 1790s known as the Tunnah Ms. that takes its name from a provincial Grand Secretary of East Lancashire. The first three Sections cover the usual Craft Degrees and a fourth Section then introduces the Super Excellent Royal Arch that includes extended catchisms on the Tabernacle, Ark of the Covenant, and the Mystery of the Cherubim. After a further Section on the full story of the Babylonian Exile and return there is the most surprising feature of all — 40 Analogies (or Comparisons) of Moses with Jesus Christ. The Ms. not only underlines the continuing Christian emphasis at the end of the century but also reveals such an amount of ritual as only those such as the Harodim could manage.

The last ritual here to be considered is one that is also very likely to have been worked in the North of England from the last decade of the 18th century.

It is the Chapter ritual in the same booklet of Alexander Dalziel that was mentioned in connection with the Passing the Chair ceremony.

What is more, this working is similar in many ways to those of Deptford and Ipswich and I therefore mainly highlight any variations.

The Janitor announces a Geometric Master Mason who has passed the Chair and now wishes 'to complete his knowledge in Masonry'. He is admitted on the Word of a Past Master of Arts and Sciences. Three Sojourners now claim ancestry from Abraham, Isaac and Jacob, and, armed with tools, they make 'a discovery' in full view of all the Companions.

A hollow space being found, the First Principal orders them to be 'well bound' and given proper refreshment for their task, so each receive a glass of wine. Moving a second keystone provides them with a parchment of the 'Holy Law' and the third withdrawal reveals a plate of gold in the form of a 'G' within which is a triangle and some undecipherable characters. These would be cypher letters.

They report to the 'Three Grand Chiefs' and Scribe Nehemiah alone confirms what they have found.

The Sojourners reclothe themselves and Z gives an emblematical explanation of what has occurred. An oration after the obligation alludes to the sprig of acacia at the grave of the 'most Excellent of all Super-excellent Masons'. Is that what Desaguliers was also alluding to on that Sunday afternoon 60 years before?

There is then a recital of the Bible story of the Jews coming from Babylon and only now is the candidate restored to light and invited to pay attention to its decoration, with a letter 'G' at its base signifying Geometric Masons.

A long charge explains how the lost word is found *and may we, my Brother Companions, preserve its margins pure and undefiled till time shall be no more*. The Chapter is then closed.

About the ceremonies of opening and closing there will be comment shortly.

The Ark of the Covenant and the 'Veils'

It was under an arch, as was mentioned much earlier, that there stood the Ark of the Covenant, the sacred chest or box that contained the relics of the ancient patriarchs.

I cannot enter here into the whole legendary background of this Ark but any who want to pursue this topic have only to read my book, *The Arch and the Rainbow* (see pp.332-338). A study of the Tunnah MS. would not come amiss.

What is important for our present study is that this Ark item reintroduces the whole caste of that Grand Lodge which formed the first part of the original material for our study.

Here we have the first Exile and its characters, Pharaoh, Moses, Aaron, Aholiab and Bezaleel, and it was as this aspect of the sacred history was recalled in at least York or the Antients Freemasonry that there appeared a series of Royal Arch steps that led from Egypt to Sinai and then to the Holy Land and Jerusalem.

We call that series of steps the Ceremony of the Veils or the Super Excellent degree and in it are displayed the call of Moses at the Burning Bush, the apparently miraculous powers of himself and Aaron, including turning a rod into a snake and back again, the erection of the tent of the Tabernacle in the wilderness and the preparation of the Ark of the Covenant for its eventual setting in the Holy of Holies in the Temple of Solomon.

We ought not to forget the pot of manna and the tablets of the Commandments which were meant to reside in the Ark.

It is not possible here to reflect at length upon this feature of early Chapter working which has now almost wholly disappeared from English practice. What does deserve some measure of thought is that for certain 18th century Royal Arch Masons it was understood why they passed from the Tabernacle in the wilderness to the eventual rebuilding of a Temple in Jerusalem.

As was hinted in the last ritual described the whole story of the intervening part of the true Master Mason's ceremony, the saga of Hiram Abi, had been purloined by the Premier Grand Lodge and used as a lesser form of Master Mason degree. When we can understand that we can truly appreciate the antiquity and integrity of the original Third Degree.

It is from this Veils ceremony that we derive the seven steps that are taken in our present practice and also some of the Scripture readings that may have seemed so out of place in our Installations of the Principals' working.

In regard to the steps, I owe it to my Jewish and Sheffield colleague, Edward Patnick, for an explanation that at last makes much sense. Three steps are those that take the pilgrim at the Jerusalem Temple from the East Gate into the outer court, then into the court of the women and next into the court of the men of Israel. The fourth and fifth steps take one into the court of the Priests and then the porchway or entrance of the inner sanctuary whilst the sixth and seventh steps take us into the Holy Place and finally the Holy of Holies itself.

The whole purpose of English Masonry is thus achieved for do we not hear in the opening of the present Third Degree: *'What inducement have you to leave the East and go to the West? To seek for that which is lost...'*

It is in the West of the Tabernacle or of the original inner Temple that the secrets of the Grand Masters were exchanged and the most sacred Word was preserved. Is it any wonder that the partially opened curtained entrance to the Holy of Holies figures so clearly on the third degree board?

Moreover, it was around this Tabernacle in the wilderness that the 12 tribes made their camp whenever they rested from their daily labours and it is from their precise positioning, as is shown in the frontispiece of the 1599 Barker Bible, that we deduce how the Chapter ensigns should now be displayed. All this as part of the Hebrews' exile experience.

The three influences which led to an 'EXILE' theme being part of the 17th century Master Mason and 18th century Royal Arch story were those of the Jewish immigrants seeking refuge here during the Lord Protector's time, the Huguenots who fled from France to Britain, and the Jacobites and Non-Jurors who took the opposite route.

Immigrants have been with us a long time.

The effect of the Huguenot membership on English Masonry cannot be too strongly stressed and the Old Testament character of our ceremonies owes not a little to them, if also to the legends reintroduced by new Jewish citizens.

Having found a safe haven in England, Ireland and Holland the Mosaic story of leaving a bondage in Egypt and reaching a promised land, along with the equally happy account of a return to Jerusalem from Babylon (Babylon, by the way, was how the Huguenots described papal Europe) explains the emphasis that was placed on the stories of Moses, Joshua, Cyrus, Zerubbabel, Ezra and Nehemiah.

These events were, as was said earlier, mentioned in the Old Charges and their history of the Craft which Dr Anderson used for his Constitutions.

Opening and Closing ceremonies

During the preceding narrative there have been several features of Royal Arch working that could not be explained in more detail at the time. They are the opening and closing of the Chapter with the origin and use of certain sacred Words, the installation of the Principals and other legends to do with a crypt.

Before we come to the close of this extensive chapter it is necessary to say something about these. If there is one aspect of Royal Arch working that represents past tradition it is the manner in which quite a number of older Chapters open and close their proceedings.

That there should have been differences between the Antients and Moderns Chapters is understandable if only because there were differences between those bodies in the way they conducted a Craft Lodge.

What I think is less to be expected is that there were even variations between the manner in which Antients Lodges acted.

To this day it is possible to find some Atholl Chapters where the only persons permitted to be in attendance when the first step of opening a Chapter is signalled are the Principals and Past Principals of that particular Chapter. The visiting Principals of whatever status, even Grand or Provincial officers, Past or current Principals of other Chapters, are requested to remain outside whilst the first part of the opening is conducted in this exclusive company.

If that seems odd it has to be reported that in one of the old West Country records there is a direction that

> 'Agreeable to the new Regulations of the Grand Royal Arch Chapter the 3 Principals only should be present at the opening; the Chapter door (being) secured, the Janitor without.'

Other, and more numerous, Chapters carry out this step with any attending Principals present and, even then, it is only when the Principals have authorised the start of the Chapter that a rubric in the ritual allows the Organist to take his place and summon the rest of the Companions by playing some martial melody.

Even in some Chapters today the Craft practice of asking questions of the various officers then takes place, including questions regarding the duties of the Principals. Moreover, especially in Yorkshire, the custom of providing the Companions of the Chapter with rods as they enter still takes place.

What is also clear from 18th century records is that whilst there were some Chapters that dismissed all but the Principals for the closing this was not as common as at the opening. It certainly appears that if there was no segregation of the members at the closing there was the involvement of all who were present in threes for the sharing of the sacred words which we are more used to seeing used by the Principals alone. This is still the normal practice in Pontefract and what makes the involvement of visitors in their making of 'threes' for sharing more difficult, is the fact that a wholly different sacred Name is the practice there.

The questioning of the officers regarding their duties at the closing was also customary and it is striking in the oldest Chapter in Hampshire that this custom includes a reading from the Epistle to the Hebrews regarding the Christian significance of the Sanctum Sanctorum.

This gradation of the opening, or its semblance of opening and closing a Craft lodge, will seem very strange to those mainly in southern areas of our country, who are accustomed to the later recommended, simpler and united form.

As the next chapter will indicate, the Holy Royal Arch in England did not at first undergo the same strict reformation after 1813 as happened to the Craft.

The Sacred Words

Whilst considering the matter of the opening and closing of a Chapter we cannot avoid the issue of the words that are, and were, associated with those parts of the ritual. In reading the most recent study of the Temple of Solomon, published in 2008, I was struck by the following passage:

> *'The ancients called their temples by names indicating that they were CHIEFLY understood to be the DWELLING PLACES of deities... Thus a temple was primarily conceived of as the earthly dwelling place of a god... and that divine presence was usually represented by an image of the deity in the most holy room in the sanctuary. Similarly, Solomons Temple was known as 'bet Yahweh' (house of Yahweh).'* (Hamblin and Seely. op. cit. p.9)

What has continually caught my attention over the years since I examined some early French rituals in Belgium and then found the reference in the Rite de Bouillon mentioned in this work, is that instead of variations of the once familiar JAHBULON a more natural and original Hebrew term was ZABULON.

This latter word translates as *'that which resides (or) dwells'* and when paired with the Sacred Name, Jehovah, describes exactly the presence of the unseen but encountered God, whom Moses met upon Mount Sinai and whose visits to the Tabernacle were marked by the cloudy Shekinah.

In view of the remarks about Solomon's Temple by the two authors above this makes sense for it was on the golden plate of the Ark of the Covenant and between the Cherubim that God was said to rest. What is quite possible is that if that was the true and original meaning its significance and its pronunciation could be misunderstood and misapplied by our Freemasonic forebears.

If this was one of the words that distinguished the true Master Masons in the 17th century and it was adopted by those like our new Huguenot, native French-speaking brethren, then it could easily have become 'Gabulon' and pronounced 'Jabulon' with interpretations that were wide of the mark. As support for this suggestion of a change from 'Z' to 'G' we should note that the name of the French battlefield was AZINCOURT but in English became AGINCOURT.

In case that suggested development might still seem somewhat far fetched I would ask you to heed once more the argument of Bro Heron Lepper as he addressed the Supreme Grand Chapter in 1933. He said:

> *'Orthography was not an accomplishment in which our Masonic forerunners excelled. I suggest that they thought more of the sound of a word than of its derivation or spelling – and if we accept this postulate, we at once get a strong family resemblance between the word of an Installed Master as we have it today,*

and the tripartite word that is divided in our Chapters. This suggestion may appear startling and fantastic, but it is not without witnesses to support it.'

To confirm his view, when Jabulon was still used, he turned their attention to three documents of the 1724-26 period. They were:

1. *A broadsheet entitled 'The Grand Mystery Laid Open' describes a Christian ritual's 'grips' in which the words used were Jachin & Boaz with the first two fingers; Gibboram & Gibberun with the wrist; and Jhimbulum & Jimbulum with the elbow.*

2. *In a Dublin broadsheet entitled 'The Whole Institution of Free-Masons Opened' he gives the words with the same grips as Jachin answered by Boaz; Magboe and Boe as answer; and Gibboram with Esimberel as reply, with the F.P.O.F. to conclude. Gibboram and Simber are later explained as the Gibeonites who built a city called Simellon.*

3. *A 1724 book called 'The Grand Mistress of the Free-Masons' in which 'Gimel' is answered by 'Nun' and then joined to give Gimel-un and later Gibelun and so Giblin.*

Bro Lepper concluded his presentation by contending that *'various essential ritual portions of the Degree of Royal Arch were known to our forerunners in England as early as the Craft Degrees themselves.'* (op. cit. Doc. 19328)

All that I would seek to claim after that is that to see the change of one letter as doubtful when it could be as varied as Gibboram, Jimbulum, Gimelun, Giblin and Jabulum, as in the 1760 French ritual, is being selective.

Of one thing I am quite convinced.

The solution of the original 'jabulon' word by Bro Castells as the Babylonian names in reverse, Anu Bel Ea, is one suggestion too far. At least we should realise that in 18th century Royal Arch Masonry they did not have the last word on this mystery.

The Installation of Principals

The issue of installing the 'Chiefs' of 18th century Chapters was also a real one.

As Bernard Jones remarks:

> *'Until the Union there was much diversity of custom with regard to the Installation of the Principals; in many Chapters the elected Principals just 'assumed the chair' without ceremony and, as was usual in the Grand Lodge of All England at York after 1761, the Craft Master, if he was qualified as a Royal Arch Mason, took the Chair as of right.'*

The Ancients may have had a similar rule.

What will again become clear in the next part of our story is that not even the Union of the Craft Grand Lodges was enough to solve this and other Chapter problems. What is certainly recorded in several sets of minutes is that even though the First Principal was installed with some ceremony his co-Principals were invested, like the other officers, by the MEZ.

As I have indicated in my book *Delving Further Beyond the Craft* (pp.53-56) the early practice of the degree of Grand High Priest, especially in Antients Lodges in Lancashire and Yorkshire, seems to have been closely connected with the Holy Royal Arch and to have provided a 'proper, mystical completion' to this Order. The apparent puzzle as to why a Priestly degree should be linked to the grade of Prince, MEZ, is solved when we learn that in the USA it was first attached to Joshua as a 1st Principal. It is now, of course, one of the Allied Degrees.

The 'Discovery' Drama

There remains to us now only one more main feature that needs our attention. It is the steady development of the crypt legends.

Mention was made earlier of the notion of an underground space beneath the Holy of Holies. In the Irish tradition, but mentioned in the quite extensive mid-18th century lectures given in the Grand Lodge of All England at York is the Biblical story of the repair of the Temple at Jerusalem by King Josiah and the discovery of the Volume of the Sacred Law by the High Priest, Hilkiah, in the Temple foundations.

What is interesting is that by the time it becomes the story of the Royal Arch for Irish Masons it has become a discovery in the crypt of the Temple as with the version selected for England.

The legends that lay behind the story of the lowering of a Sojourner, who is not always, the Principal Sojourner, as in Scotland, into a domed vault, are two in number.

The first story became available in a book, *Orbis Miraculum*, published in 1659, and Bernard Jones comments on it thus:

> 'Even a casual study of this now rare and famous book can scarcely fail to give the impression that the framers of the early Royal Arch ceremonial had access to it, and drew inspiration not only from its text but from its frontispiece that shows a Prince and High Priest in what could be Chapter robes holding a banner with the title of the book.'

The prince was Solomon and the priest was Zadok, who helped to carry the Ark of the Covenant. The two Bible quotations on the cover concern the coming up of the tribes of Israel from Chaldea or Babylon and a word from St. John on Patmos on sacrifices acceptable to God.

The legend contained in this book is that of Philostorgius in the early 4th century AD.

It tells how in the course of repairs to Jerusalem by the Emperor Julian a cave was by chance revealed and a workman let down by a rope found a room perfectly square and a pillar with a book wrapped in linen upon it. This proved to be the whole Gospel of John in his tongue.

Another legendary version was that of Callistus and though it has various detailed differences its main thrust is the act of lowering a workman to discover a cave with its contents revealed.

Rather different is the story in the Book of Enoch which mentioned a site in the mountains of Canaan where eight vaults, each one below the other, finally revealed the true name of God in a golden triangle.

Before we leave this sacred, if also legendary, underground area there is one more feature of earlier provenance that must be mentioned. It was the presence near to, or around, the pillar in the vault of a representation of a Zodiac cycle of symbolic creatures.

Indeed, in Scotland there are still many extant vaults, or their models, which are always decorated in this way. For those who might wish to learn more about this aspect of early Freemasonry, and not least why it is no longer part of our Chapter furniture, there is my Batham Lecture, *'The Path of the Zodiac in Royal Arch Masonry'* which can be obtained on application to the author. Why it figured so consistently in 18th century working and then disappeared is an intriguing story in itself.

Further understanding of the rope or cord used in the search of the vault almost certainly leads us back to the instructions contained in the Mishnah, an ancient commentary on Jewish history.

Here, we are told that when the High Priest entered the Holy of Holies on the Day of Atonement, Yom Kippur, he passed through the veils of the door in the West and at once found himself in total darkness, in a windowless chamber shaped like a perfect cube. Since no-one else was ever permitted to accompany him there he was provided with a lifeline so that, should he faint or expire during his sojourn in this sacred shrine, he could be drawn out by two priests who stood outside and who held the ends of the cord that encircled him.

Similarly, that record informs us that if he wished to move about or withdraw, being overcome with noxious vapours, he was able to signal by pulling on the left or right of the cord. From such august sources do our practices take their rise.

Here then, is yet another instance of how, when we recognise and share the wide, remarkable and ancient knowledge that our forebears had available and acquired, we can better appreciate the route this Order took towards its present shape.

We are the beneficiaries of a great heritage.

The Routeless Royal Arch? 1813-1834

There is one part of our Royal Arch journey which has never before, to my knowledge, been told in detail.

It is the examination of the varying practices of some of the Chapters that were in existence in the first 20 years after 1813. Only as we appreciate more fully the problems and attitudes of Chapter Masons at this period are we able to understand why in 1834 decisive steps were taken to re-establish the Royal Arch on a clearer course and with a firm basis.

Before I come to the detail of what we can cover in one chapter, however, we must consider the larger picture that embraces this period.

That the 1813 Union of the Premier and Antients Grand Lodges was necessary and right is beyond doubt. The establishing of clear guidelines for the Craft both at home and in the emerging British Empire was essential and the Duke of Sussex rightly bent all his efforts to make sure that the Craft side of the Union agreement was directed with care. He may have thought that by including the Royal Arch as an 'Order' in the description of Ancient Freemasonry he was preserving the right of that aspect of Masonry to continue its course. Yet there were some problems created in this regard by the new Union.

As nothing but the first three degrees and the Installation could now be permitted in a Craft lodge what was a Lodge like that of St Luke, Ipswich, expected to do, for its records show that Chapter work was being done in the Lodge 10 years after the Union? If Past Masters were not any longer automatically the Principals of a Chapter how were such officers chosen?

Again, what was the requirement for entry to this new Order, because previous Atholl lodges still insisted on a candidate having passed the Chair whereas some Moderns chapters only required such a qualification for the three Principals' chairs? Furthermore, if a Chapter was no longer attached to a particular Lodge, could candidates be accepted from anywhere?

Just as important was the question, of whether it was still really a DEGREE, even if it was called an Order, and what clothing were Royal Arch Masons to wear now that in the Craft they were required to use their own specific dress? Mention of just these few issues, and there were several others, will perhaps explain why I named this chapter as I did.

Granted that the Craft was now under new management and direction, where was the Royal Arch going and in what manner?

In a very real sense there was at this time little common agreement on how the organisation or ceremonies of the Royal Arch were to be managed.

Bro Cyril Batham once put the situation clearly:

'The Grand Chapter of the Moderns was a separate entity and, as such, was unaffected by the merger. The so-called Grand Chapter of the Antients was an integral part of its Grand Lodge and therefore went out of existence on 27 December 1813 when its Grand Lodge did so… As a result there was a marked falling off in recorded Exaltations, from 848 in 1812 to 389 in 1813… to 132 in 1816… Had Laurence Dermott still been alive it is quite definite that he would have made sure the Antients had more control over the future of the Royal Arch degree. It seems almost as though, once they had persuaded the Moderns to recognise the Royal Arch, they lost interest in it… and certainly it seems that their Royal Arch administration more or less fell apart. There is no record of their ever having made contact with the Grand Chapter of the Moderns.' (Collected Papers, pp.95f.)

There were, as we shall see, two occasions, in 1817 and 1825, when attempts were made in London to give some direction to the Order but the varied reactions to those steps will, as we shall also see, only suggest the more how rudderless the Royal Arch seems to have been. But what, we now need to note, is actually what happened.

From the history of St James Chapter No. 2 in London we note that the Chapter used to open from 3–5pm, then called off to dine, still using a central table in the meeting room, and resumed at 8pm. In 1814 they continued the same practice, only meeting from 4–6pm, adjourned for refreshments, and resumed at 9pm, after which and for the FIRST TIME, the Chapter closed in what is now called SOLEMN form.

A year later it is noted that three lectures were now to be given regularly, so presumably this had not been the custom before. It is also worth noting that the Chapter's Bylaws state that to be accepted as a Companion meant simply being *'a MM proved'* though this is not what we shall notice elsewhere.

The well-known Mason, Walter Rodwell Wright, a close friend of the Prince Regent, was in the Z chair in 1814 and had been for at least five years. He was succeeded by E.Comp. Burckhardt for two years, and then William Williams, the Grand Superintendent of Dorset, was MEZ for 10 years. There was clearly no accepted rule about how long one remained in the Chairs, here or elsewhere, and we recall that there was certainly no set rule about the Installation of Principals.

In 1817, the compromise amalgamation of the bodies that had once overseen the Moderns and Antients Royal Arch working led to changes in this Chapter. The MEZ referred to the most important regulation passed by this new Supreme Grand Chapter which was the need to attach their Chapter to a 'respectable' Lodge and hence they chose Antiquity No. 2.

They thus became aware of the Antients Royal Arch working that was noticeably different to their own and so they combined the two in a form agreed by the members. This in turn meant that they needed a different method of testing visitors.

From 1818, a Chapter Committee was also set up to consider how the Principals should be installed and this was the procedure followed until the Chapter of Promulgation of 1825 issued a new form which was adopted by this Chapter for the rest of the century.

Their acceptance of direction in this quarter was not to be the more general rule. In 1822, their own new forms of regalia and jewels were agreed by the Chapter and in 1829 their inventory includes a Throne, a platform, pillars, drapery and a 'Glory', with four chairs for the PZs with, note this, *'irons to steady them'*. Was that, I wonder, because the occupants were so obese? In this London Chapter, there is a sense of steady change but they at least keep meeting regularly.

A similar pattern of regular meeting is at first found in the minutes of the Chapter of Nativity No. 126 in Burnley, Lancashire. This Chapter's name, like Cana, that of its neighbour *'just up the road'* at Colne, recall for us the decidedly Christian catechisms that first provided early Chapter ritual.

Here, at Burnley, we have the complete minutes for this period and the tally of candidates is striking;

Four in 1812; three in 1813; five in 1815; 16 in 1817; and then 15 in the next five years. However, after that there are only six in the next 13 years. Not only was there this drop in numbers of 'exHaltees' (as candidates are so recorded in many Lancashire Chapters) but also in the frequency of their meetings.

The Rules at the start of their Minute Book state that the Chapter will meet on the 2nd SUNDAY each MONTH and then make clear that *'Candidates for this degree* (and 'degree' is the term used by them throughout this period) *must have conducted themselves with propriety through all the degrees of Craft Masonry and have the unanimous consent of all those present'*.

Contrary to the St James's Chapter's rule this meant that if Master Masons wished to join they had to be Installed Masters or to have taken the ceremony of 'passing the Chair'. Indeed, the practice of 'passing the Chair', though officially discouraged from the 1820s, was still being practised in this parent Lodge of the Silent Temple 30 years later, when 13 brethren were so passed.

What is very clear is the variety of terms used here to name the degree.

In 1812, a Brother is proposed *'as an ADVOCATE for the Royal Arch'*. In 1813, two brethren *'are duly honoured with the FELLOWSHIP of Companion of the Royal Arch'*, by 1814 two more candidates are proposed *'to become a MOST EXCELLENT (sic) or Royal Arch Mason'*, and in 1822 the candidates *'are EXCEPTED (sic) and made Royal Arch or Excelent (sic)'*. The guard of the Chapter is throughout called TYLOR but whereas this post had previously been held annually by a Chapter member it is decided in May 1813 to have a paid Tylor who was to receive either 1/- for each meeting OR one glass of Ale or spirits. In the next month they approve a plan for certain *'candlesticks to be made according to the principles laid down by the MEMBERS'*. In the absence of nationwide rules we see them, as in London, exercising self-help.

It is noticeable that summonses were not normal here and were only issued for the following:

the October meeting when Z., who was himself elected, chose his officers;

for any emergency occasions; or when quarterly dues were to be paid.

In 1816, there is an unusual entry, which reveals the confused relationship with their parent Lodge of the Silent Temple. It reads:

'The Chapter to go on meeting on Sundays but 5/6d of each Initiation fee for the Royal Arch to be allowed to the Craft but 1 guinea to be paid by the Craft to the Royal Arch on admission to a Craft degree.'

If that sounds odd to you, as it does to me, it only serves to show how necessary it was becoming to have new general regulations.

In 1817, when the Royal Arch systems of the Antients and Moderns were officially amalgamated, we read here on August 10:

'Bro. Hodgson was not EXHALTED on account of a new Code of Law received on 3rd Inst. Resolved that Laws & Regulations received from Grand Chapter be put in full force with an additional rule that non-payment of ½ year's dues by the year's end would mean exclusion.'

They too were recognising the need for more direction.

Acceptance of the new rules mentioned probably explains why in March 1818 the Chapter sent a letter to the Grand S.E. complaining that at Bottoms, near Halifax, the Chapter there was making Royal Arch Masons illegally.

The Minutes at Bottoms do indeed confirm that since 1811, when that Chapter moved to Bottoms from Haworth, it was usual for a Brother to receive the Old Mark degree as part of the Craft with the degrees of Ark, Mark and Link often also conferred at that point. The degree of Super Excellent Mason, or the Veils, was considered part of a Royal Arch ceremony.

That this was still the case in 1833 is confirmed by the fact that the Cana Chapter, Colne, to which we shall shortly turn, decided in that year to adopt this method of conducting the Royal Arch. What is noteworthy for us is that despite the Burnley complaint no action was taken, presumably because there were no established means of regulating Royal Arch affairs nationally and in England central bodies have not, as we have seen recently, insisted too much on ritual uniformity.

It is interesting, for example, that in December 1818 the Burnley Companions sought a dispensation to permit two brethren who had not been Master Masons 12 months to be Exalted. They received no guidance at all from London.

A comment here from Bro Bernard Jones is apt:

'For some years following the Union, Royal Arch Masonry was in a somewhat chaotic condition. The records of a great many minute-books go to show that letters addressed to Grand Chapter were neglected, returns often unacknowledged and, perhaps as a result, failing to be made punctually in later years' with the effect that centenaries were distressingly delayed. (Book of the Royal Arch p.119).

In December 1820, the Burnley Companions decided that their Chapter needed a ballot box and balls. This was probably since the previous close relations with the Lodge were beginning to deteriorate and so separate items of this kind would be necessary.

In 1821, it is noted that a hammer (only one?) was donated for use by the Chiefs, the Lodge mallets presumably being no longer available, and 24 new aprons were to be provided. This latter step shows that as the Craft now required their own style of apron the Chapter had to have other regalia.

Pursuing this theme it was resolved in December 1823 that the Sojourners should now have

'clothing suitable to their office' whilst in April 1824 '6 kid leather aprons were to be supplied for the 3 Sojourners and 3 Past Principals according to the Articles'.

That there was a growing wish to have clear direction is shown by a letter to Grand Chapter in June 1822 asking about how Royal Arch warrants were to be provided, but when they want guidance as to whether they can move from the Cross Keys Inn the Companions approach the Craft P.G.M.

Some kind of directive seems to have begun for in 1825 they start to sign the Minutes and in 1827 there is the new formula, 'The Chapter was opened in REGULAR form and with SOLEMN prayer.' This was more than 10 years after the same procedure in St James Chapter, London.

At this point the Chapter was affected by problems in the Craft Lodge that led to the Lodge's suspension from May 1828 to September 1830. During this period there are no Chapter Minutes because the Chapter furniture and Charter had been removed to the Royal Oak Inn. What is to be noted in the Lodge history is the comment: *'The Lodge had removed and thought the Chapter should do so also, on the ground that it was attached to, and inseparable from, the Lodge.'* (p. 35)

Direction on such matters from a higher authority was clearly needed.

Though there is mention of both the preparatory and historical lectures now being given, though not three as you may recall being adopted in 1814 in London, the fact is that from 1831 meetings in Burnley become noticeably fewer.

Meanwhile along the road in Colne at the Cana Chapter, matters also took their own individual course. Meetings, as at Burnley, were held on a SUNDAY and the election of the Masters, which was the name used by them for the Principals, always took place on Trinity Sunday. Readers will surely be fully aware by now why such a date had been chosen.

From June 1813 to April 1814, no meetings took place but in the latter month a Robert Horner is raised *'from the Chair to be initiated a Royal Arch Mason'* and in May, Chair Masons were raised to the Illustrious Order of the Royal Arch or of Excellent Masons and 'the Chapter closed in harmony HAS (sic) Excellent Companions'. Wording and spelling was far from fixed.

There were regular meetings until 1822 but only one or two 'raisings' (note, NOT 'exaltations') each year and the Minutes in June 1818 are at last being signed. In 1815, the first proposal for Jewels is made, as also for a new floorcloth, and in 1816 a search was made for their warrant. In June 1821, only three Officers are named.

One wonders if this Chapter would survive.

From May 1822, an agreement was minuted to have meetings every OTHER month and in January 1825, *'not having Members SUFFISHANT the Companions went through Part of the LECTOR and then Enjoy(ed) themselves with a Glass'* with the Chapter not appearing to have been closed.

We now regularly read the words *'the Lecter (sic) gone throu'* and in November this took place *'in the PRESANTS (sic) of the 3 Most Excellent Grand Masters'. The 2 Scribes and 2 Sojourners (are) fined for being absent'*. Fines, by the way, abound in this Chapter.

It might be worth noting that in the back of their Cash Book there is recorded the Resolution of the London Quarterly Communication of August 2nd, 1826, that *'No Companion of a Subordinate Chapter shall be eligible for the Principals Chairs unless he be Master or Past Master of a Craft Lodge. Promotion to those Chairs must be by occupying the J, H.& then Z. chairs.'*

Presumably some Chapters had been trying to cut corners.

In December, they decided that *'a sumond (sic) was to be sent so that proper arrangements could be made for Regulation of this Chapter'* and there are clearer signs of what they now do. The *'Making Parts, the Lector and Estorical parts of the Order wear then gone throu'*.

From 1828 it was also agreed that the By-laws be read every other month; that a list of members be sent to the Grand Superintendent; and that they now use the term 'Janitor'.

Even so, as was referred to earlier, the members were now invited to come to Bottoms to see their form of working in a Chapter, with dinner and a glass provided. How could one refuse that? The result was that by May 1829 it was decided that the Bottoms Companions should come on Trinity Sunday and *'give us Super Excellent (degree) &c'*.

After this date we read of them opening their Chapter in *'ANCIENT and solemn form'*, of surplices and caps being paid for and a Super Excellent degree being conferred. We even read of one Companion joining this Chapter so as to receive this latter step.

When we reach their minutes in 1835 it is to note that a Companion is asked to go to London to see a new style of Chapter working. At last there is some clearer direction.

Before we move to see what was happening in other parts of the country it may be as well if we refresh our minds with what the state of the ritual was at this point.

As will have become clear from what has already been noted, the requirement of a candidate *'having passed the Craft Chair'* was normal and so, if the candidate did not have this qualification, some of the Chapter members formed a temporary Lodge to repair that deficiency.

That accomplished, the 'Ceremony of the Veils' may follow though that was not done on every occasion. If it was omitted then the candidate would be taken through them on a later occasion.

The Chapter would then be opened with an esoteric exchange between the Principals which might be, as convenient, in a separate room or quietly in the East. The catechism of the officers would follow, and, as still happens in some Yorkshire Chapters, the Sojourners report themselves as the guardians of the separate Veils, whether or not that ceremony had taken place.

There was then a much longer prayer by J. and an exhortation by Z. which specifically included mention of that *'sprig of cassia found on the grave of the most excellent of Masons'*, or *'the beautiful rose of Sharon'* and *'the lily of the valley'* which to a perceptive Christian ear would suggest the true identity of the noble Grand Master who was slain. The very fact that these terms did not persist in use after 1835 supports the view that for the older Royal Arch Mason more than Hiram, the widow's son, was involved.

What this kind of ceremony also did was to keep in mind for the Companions the close connection between the old Moses, Solomon and Zerubbabel sections of the rite because, recognised now as Sojourners, the candidate, or candidates, were presented with the 'discovery in the vault' and then a report to their Excellencies as today, with the reward of the investiture explanations.

There would then be some five more 'lectures' (lectors, lecters) which might, or might not, be given in full or given when there was no candidate present.

Those readers who might like to see what was in these lectures can do so by consulting Richard Carlile's *Manual of Freemasonry* (pp. 109ff).

Moving further north to Durham we note that the Chapter of Concord No.51, held in the Granby Lodge room, Old Elvet, was working under a warrant of Dispensation granted by Thomas Dunckerley in 1791.

Following a period of inactivity we read in November 1821, the following petition from them, obviously revealing the need for more support:

'...having the prosperity of our Grand and Universal Science at heart, (we) are anxious to exert our pure & best endeavours to promote and diffuse the genuine

principles of our Royal Sublime Art'. And so request a renewal of the earlier Warrant to meet on every 4th Tuesday (note: NOT Sunday):

'to discharge the duties of our exalted degree'. There were 13 members.

We note from the returns to the Grand Scribe E that there had been three exaltations in 1809, one in 1810, one in 1811 and two in 1818, but no minutes are extant before 1822. The Chapter was clearly in need of stability.

In the first record of January 1822 we get a flavour of how work was carried out in this particular Chapter. The Craft Lodge Certificate was read out aloud before the ballot and the candidate being found favourable was exalted and then admitted a Companion of this Excellent, GRAND & Royal Chapter.

The MEZ then delivered parts of the Lecture *'ILLUSTRATIVE of the Ceremony'*. This latter note indicates that what were being used were the series of lectures that were virtual resumés of what had taken place in the ceremony. It was these lectures, like the ones preserved by Finch and Carlile, that were to be replaced with those with which we are familiar.

All seemed to be going swimmingly with Exaltees in February and March but when it was stated that the Chapter would be CLOSED to the last THURSDAY in MAY some might have thought that there was a problem.

There was. The minutes of March 1822 were not read until two years later. The Right Worshipful Master, the Chaplain and two other brethren of the Granby Lodge were then exalted together, whilst on the 29th of the same month, two more brethren 'having passed the Chair' were Exalted. There is never any sign of a dispensation for such action.

It is also February 1825 before there is any mention of a special day for the appointment of officers. There were no candidates for the next six months but the MEZ always gave the Lecture and goes 'through the illustration of the Grand Ceremony'. When two candidates are at last proposed it is for *'exaltation to this SUBLIME Degree'*.

This Chapter clearly holds on to its old description of the Royal Arch as a degree, Union or no Union. That the Chapter appreciated the work of the MEZ in *'Instructing them in the Lecture and Illustration'* is marked by their presentation to him of a Sash of the Order. Yet following this presentation there are times when, though there might be an Exaltation, there was no Lecture.

After a gap of another year it was decided that officers should be elected each year. The same pattern is repeated in 1833 but in September that year the next Principals are in fact Installed in their Chairs by their predecessors.

The Chapter approved the purchasing of robes for these officers, even though six months later they still do not seem to have acquired either them or *'the other paraphernalia necessary and proper for the Chapter'*. It is only after another gap of 16 months that some kind of stability seems to be emerging.

In October 1835 officers are elected, the Principals are Installed and following his beautiful lecture explaining the Grand Pedestal, Comp. Townsend *favoured the*

Chapter with some remarks on the antiquity and beauties of Freemasonry'. A letter was then read out inviting the Principals to witness the new ceremonies in London and it was reported that E.Comp.Thompson had attended Grand Chapter in May and been Installed by the new method.

The Principal Sojourner, Comp.R.Robson, also attended in June to see the new ceremony of Exaltation. It was Comp.Thompson who a year later paid 13 guineas for the robes and other items. The Scribes now had crimson scarves, such as are still worn in the Chapter of Justice at Derby, and the Principals now had signs on their staves. The Past Masters (the same term as used in Colne) had robes faced with light blue, trimmed with sable fur.

Now turning southwards we have the Chapter of Vigilance in Darlington with records that cover the whole of this period.

In 1812, the Chapter is functioning with *'3 Principles (sic) and 4 Companions in July, a Bro. Brown exalted in October and in December the 3 Sojourners are elected'* and it was agreed that on Christmas Day there would be a 'beef stake' on the menu. On that day itself there were 14 Companions expected but 15 came and they paid 1/- for their food.

The next year they cancelled two meetings but they had two candidates in April of whom one 'Passed the Chair' and in May there was another, and in August and October they gave the Lectures. Meanwhile in June and December they chose three more as Principals while, when another Passed the Chair in November, they announced that the Christmas 'beef' would cost 1/6d.

They met the next month to make By-laws and two days later all the members signed them.

They did not have enough attendees to meet until June when the Lodge, Concord, went to Barnard Castle and Passed a Brother through the Chair.

In September, they asked for the surplices to be washed. They once more ordered beef for Christmas but though 15 booked in only nine attended. This was indicating a loss of support because they did not meet again till May 1815 for the Lectures and then no gathering till December when it was discovered that the Books had been mislaid and hence no minutes or summonses.

In 1816, they met only for lectures in March and November though they did have their beef-stake on December 31 at the Installing of the three Principals. They met in February and March but then nothing, until 18 were present at the December dinner.

On 3May 1818, they passed some through the Chair to take the 'Most Excellent Degree of the Royal Arch'. That year they ate beef also on St John the Baptist's day in June, at 8pm and for 12 Companions.

There were many adjournments of meetings though they made new Principals in April 1819 and on Christmas Day that year they could invite any member of the Restoration Lodge to dinner.

When they met next in September 1821, the Chapter was opened 'in Ancient form' and it was reported that the Chapter jewels that had been taken by the Janitor had been returned, though they were still waiting for the Certificates from the Grand Chapter which were paid for.

In 1820, the ceremony was now called the Holy Royal Arch, Passing the Chair still took place and the Tyler of the Lodge was Exalted so that he could act as Janitor. In 1822, the meetings began to be held on a Sunday but the following year the Chapter wrote to London complaining that they did not appear in the official list of Chapters nor had they received any Quarterly Communications.

A new Grand Superintendent appears in 1825 and asks for a list of members but sadly numbers now decline and there were only three meetings from July until the following January at which point it was announced that there would be *'no meetings till further notice'*.

There were two meetings for 'lectures' around the New Year of 1828 but then nothing till December 1829 when there were just three Principals, three Companions and the Janitor. Their full complement was 10 members.

They again did not meet from February to August 1830 and though it was reported that there was an *'Excellent lecture'* in January 1831, no-one met until June and a mere six times before a Candidate appears, in June 1834.

They met for lectures in October, a NEW Warrant at last arrived, and at last in early 1835 the signs of a new direction appeared. The ribbon for new sashes was ordered and it was decided that all the existing members should be provided with an Apron and Sash. Two *'gentlemen candidates'* appear, though by 1837 they were still carrying out the passing the Chair ceremony and buying items for the Veils ceremony.

It is now time to take a look at what was happening in Sheffield and Doncaster and the Midlands.

In Sheffield there were three Chapters at this period with much information about their practice.

The Chapter of Loyalty minutes state that on 17 January 1813, *'a GENERAL ENCAMPMENT of R.A. Masons was held at which the MEZ gave the Charge, the Lectures, &c (sic) and then adjourned until the 3rd Sun in Feb.'*

The term *'encampment'* was used regularly until 1821 and again in 1823 and was used by Sheffield brethren as they helped start the Magdalen Chapter in Doncaster. Whilst it may seem a somewhat unusual term to us it does of course represent the reality of the Hebrew tribes settling down each night in the wilderness in an encampment formation as represented by the original biblical layout of the ensigns.

In August 1813, we read that the Sheffield Chapter was *'closed in due form, after which a great part of the Lecture was given by Z and THE Sojourner'* whilst in December 1814 Bros Jepson and Hudson, *'having passed the Superlative Chair, were exalted'*.

In January, four Companions were made MARK Masons in the Chapter and in May there was no business, but they chatted over victuals about how to have a procession to celebrate the Union of Antients and Moderns. This at least shows us that the earlier form of meeting round a table was still followed.

In February 1817, ballot balls were issued to decide whether a Bro Wilson could be admitted as a visitor. It appears that he was Exalted so long ago that he had forgotten the signs. In April they opened, had three lectures, closed but, as the candidate was late because his coach was delayed, they opened AGAIN and Exalted him.

In 1820, an order was given for new headdresses for the Principals, a visitor from Britannia Lodge explained the floorcloth, tracing board and jewels, whilst in November there was an agreement that Companions should now dress in black, have a PROPER apron, a sash and gloves. What a proper apron was at this point is anyone's guess.

However, in 1821, the Chapter acquired a new warrant and new name. It was now the Chapter of Paradise. Paradise, however, was short lived. After 1822, its name became The Royal Brunswick Chapter and that too was closed in 1829 and did not reopen until 1861.

Of Alfred and Sincerity Chapters in Sheffield, time prevents me from saying anything further than that they met more fitfully, albeit for a longer period.

In Doncaster, in 1812, the Royal Arch was in a parlous state.

The Minutes for 10 May state that

> 'At a General Encampment... there not being a sufficient Number of Companions at Doncaster to open a Chapter, the 15 names in the margin belonging to (members of) the Chapter of Paradise, Sheffield, were requested to open this Chapter which they did in due form. 17 Masons were then approved to the Supreme degree of Royal Arch Companions with an appropriate Lecture'.

The older practice of requiring a separate fee for membership of the Chapter was still followed and only current members of St George's Lodge could so apply.

Many meetings had insufficient present for a Chapter to be formed and in an attempt to attract members the fee was temporarily reduced from three guineas to one, whilst absence from Chapter for three consecutive nights incurred a fine of 2/6d. As in the Colne Chapter fines were frequent.

After a more steady year when attendances were from 10 to 15, the meeting in April 1818 was the last for five years. Even when the Chapter resumed it was for only one gathering a year and then with too few members to form a regular Chapter. The letters from Grand Chapter requesting fees were unanswered.

On Sunday 22 July, 1827, there was an evident sense of new life. Five new members were proposed and they were to be balloted for at the next meeting in August. On that occasion they met at Jesus College Chapter in Rotherham where one of the candidates *'went through the degree of P.M. before lunch and then was exhalted to the Superior degree of Royal Arch Mason'*.

The fascinating thing about this entry is that they had agreed in July *'that the order of Grand Chapter respecting exhaltation should be punctually and strictly obeyed'*. This seems to mean that being an Installed Master was still a usual requirement.

The Chapter met at the Mansion House, Guild Hall and the Town Hall successively but meetings in 1828 were attracting up to 19 Companions. In 1829, the ceremony is now called, as in Sheffield, the SUPERLATIVE degree and this title persists for the rest of the year.

In January 1831, we read that *'the Grand LODGE be written to, to request that they would forward the Laws of the Constitution (since the Union) of the Royal Arch Degree'* and this, we should remember, had been in 1817, and they continue, *'also that (the Grand Lodge) would no longer delay forwarding the Royal Arch Certificates PAID FOR HERETOFORE, and written for so repeatedly...'*

In October of that year there is a minute *'requesting that any brother going to London would be kind enough to call at the Grand Secretaries (sic) Office and ask for the Rules of the Constitution of the Royal Arch'*. Communication with the centre was still far from good.

A special meeting was held on Wednesday (not the usual Sunday) July 11, 1832, when Comp. Lockwood was proposed as MEZ in place of the recently deceased E.Comp. Welbourne, who had been a Principal since 1813 and MEZ from 1827.

Rules about the length of tenure of office were not known or applied, as we have seen elsewhere.

When it was proposed, say the minutes *'of the last Lodge' (sic)*, that E.Comp. Lockwood be replaced as MEZ after only a year he at once resigned. Well, we all know what can happen when expected traditions are changed.

By 1834, the numbers attending were too small to permit a regular Chapter to meet and apart from one meeting with ten Companions on Tuesday, 15 April, no Chapter was held until 1839. A sense of insubstantial Royal Arch Masonry persisted.

A similar sense of uncertainty and lack of direction is evident from the surviving evidence of Atholl Lodge No. 199, at Dewsbury where, as we would expect, their 1794 regulations affirm the right of the Lodge, under its warrant, to conduct the *'fourth degree'* in Masonry, for which passage through the Craft chair was a requirement. We can thus assume that that Chapter had a life at Dewsbury until 1820 when the lodge moved to Honley.

As there is then no mention of 'Passing the Chair' in the Lodge minutes the fate of the Royal Arch for six years is unknown. However, when the Lodge moved to Meltham in 1826 references to the officially banned ceremony recur until 1830, so it is likely that the Royal Arch was still practised in the new home of Lodge of Peace No. 149. This disjointed story tells its own tale.

The Chapter of Justice had been dormant in Nottingham for many years when a Grand Chaplain and a local Vicar were able to obtain a personal dispensation from H.R.H. the Duke of Sussex in 1815 permitting the Chapter to remove to Derby.

Since the Tyrian Lodge, to which this Chapter was now to be attached, had, though under the Moderns, previously worked the Royal Arch by reason of its Lodge warrant, it was now told in a letter from the Duke's secretary that they

> *'may consider the enclosed dispensation a high mark of H.R.H's condesencion (sic) and favour; nor is it wish'd so to be spoken of, as in any way to be taken as a precedent whereon to grant similar applications...'*

Rule by private favour was here the name of the game. The Derby warrant was endorsed in 1816 but when the rule was introduced in 1817 that every Chapter must be attached to a Craft Lodge this Derby Chapter was so unorganised that it was 1822 before a return was made. What happened after that date is unknown as their extant minutes do not start until 1848.

In Nottingham, after 1813, the actual situation of the Royal Arch was uncertain.

Those Antients who had been Exalted remained Royal Arch Masons but were now bereft of a ruling body. Since the United Grand Lodge did not permit a working of the Royal Arch in its Lodges, a Lodge which did so was acting under dubious authority.

By the wording of Article II of the Act of Union the Antients had claimed a victory for their beliefs yet they had conceded that control of the H.R.A. would be detached from the United Grand Lodge without ensuring the creation of a new ruling body. They had also accepted that the Royal Arch degree would no longer be the fourth degree.

The situation at this time therefore was that Abbey Lodge, having been an Antients Lodge, had to spawn a separate Chapter as it could no longer work the Royal Arch under a Lodge warrant and there was no royal favour here.

We know that the Craft Lodge permitted 92 brethren to 'Pass the Chair' in 25 years, 1798-1823, and their last such ceremony recorded was, as in Burnley, after the practice had been officially ended. How many of these Masons were in fact Exalted, or where, we do not know but it does suggest that some Royal Arch activity locally was continued.

Certainly we know of two Exaltations in 1830 and 1832 but then the lost minutes are again a block to more helpful research. It can now perhaps be seen why study of this period has attracted such little attention.

In Cambridge, the record claims that the Chapter *'has carefully preserved the traditions and workings it received at its consecration'*. This latter took place at the Hoop Hotel in April, 1828 when a Master's Lodge was opened and the purpose of the day declared after which the dedicating of a new Chapter was conducted by no less a figure than the Revd George Adam Browne, the chairman of the later Revision Committee, as the first M.E.Z.

The first Chapter opening was by the Most Excellent Companions and Principals ONLY after which the other Companions were admitted. In the Charter, Browne is described as *'His Most Excellent Sir Rev...'* The three Principals then proceeded to *'constitute, establish and engraft a Chapter'*.

Brethren were then *'exalted to the honourable distinction of Comps'* (p. 12). The assembled Companions took refreshment and then those not through the Chair withdrew whilst the elected Principals were Installed. On their return the other Companions saluted the Principals *'with becoming respect'*. The Principal Sojourner then *'exercised his privilege of appointing his two assistants'*.

In 1829, THREE candidates were Exalted although one at each meeting in 1828. In April 1831, eight candidates were Exalted thus showing great new interest. The custom of opening a Craft Lodge after Chapter was still being followed. There was then a lapse of two years and another eight were Exalted in 1833.

In 1835, the Grand Superintendent announced changes in the ceremony of Exaltation and enlarged upon, and explained, these changes. When three Brethren were admitted for Exaltation the Grand Superintendent also addressed them on the ceremonies, their nature and origin, and also explained the Jewels in Royal Arch Masonry.

It may interest Companions today to note that not only were seven Masons Exalted as part of the inaugural proceedings but the new Companions of the Pythagoras Chapter were addressed with ten lines of verse in classical Latin. The Companions, record the minutes, then sought refreshment (perhaps not surprisingly) before the Principals were PRIVATELY Installed and then they appointed their officers. To round off an unusual occasion the Chapter was *'ingrafted upon the Scientific Lodge No. 131 as a continuation of a 4th degree'*.

Moreover, the Chapter being closed, an Entered Apprentice Lodge *'was opened so as to afford members of the Craft Lodge the opportunity of dining with the Companions. The Provincial Grand Superintendent took his departure about ten o'clock and the Lodge was closed shortly after'*.

Since dining in Lodge was meant to have ended after 1813 it might seem somewhat surprising to read such a record had we not already heard that they did the same in Sheffield, Doncaster and London.

Considering how often the above Chapters were meant to meet it is revealing that in Cambridge they only met three times a year. Even so, circumstances prevented the Chapter meeting in 1830 and 1832 and thereafter they met only once a year.

Was it only coincidence that it was E.Comp. Adam Browne who sought to form the future styles of Chapter ritual and government? He must have realised that some general help and regulation was now needed.

It was in 1793 when the Domatic Chapter in London began its working separately from the Lodge but the first Warrant was on 29 October 1810.

Its heading then was Atholl Chapter 234 dated A.D. 1793. The number was changed to 293 in 1813, when the Domatic Lodge was in conflict with any who were about to effect the Union.

The Lodge members opposed certain ritual alterations which may have been parts of the ceremonies that touched upon the Royal Arch.

A new register was considered necessary by the Grand Chapter after 1817, and those Chapters not attached to a Lodge were to take steps to bring this about. The 'Deomatic Chapter' (sic) members asked to continue being attached to the Domatic Lodge and to meet on the second Sunday in every month. This was agreed in October 1818.

Henry Sadleir, the historian, and then the Grand Janitor, regularly attended this Chapter as a visitor. He spent much of his time visiting Chapters to see that the proceedings were properly carried out. The minutes before 1845 have been lost but there is a book in leather called 'Dom. Chap. of H.R.A. Treasurer's Accounts' from 27 May 1827 to March 1932.

From 1829 to 1836, the title changes to 'Domatic Chapter of United Strength'. The latter was not due to a loyal use of the term 'United' after the Union but to a further opposing Lodge called '399 Lodge of United Strength'.

It had been my plan to include more examples of this period from East Anglia, the mid-South and South-west but on enquiry I was informed that such places as Norwich, Exeter, and Plymouth lost many records owing to wartime damage. There is, however, the invaluable book by Joseph Osborn on Freemasonry in West Cornwall and that provides us with the story of the Druids Chapter, Redruth, for this same period.

Their story at this time begins with an enquiry in 1812 about three Sceptres and 12 banners similar to those in St James Chapter, which is where we began this survey.

In 1813 they had no Exaltations. In 1814, however, they met three times and had five Exaltations of professional and wealthy men, but 1815 had no meetings and the Chapter seems to have been in trouble. By 1816, they were able to receive two gentlemen and a General.

In 1818, they had three candidates; an innkeeper, a merchant and another 'Esquire' and in April 1819 a new Chapter Journal was started. They had three Exaltations, and both in April and August they distinguish themselves by making charitable donations to Brethren from as far afield as Ireland, London, and Manchester. The Chapter is now described as opening and closing in Solemn Form with Prayer.

There was another Exaltation in 1821 but no more until 1826, though we have the request for a repair to 'Jeshua's cap' which proves that the Principals had robes and hats, and there was a sad note that one of their members was refused entry to Grand Chapter as not being registered on their books. This led to a warm exchange of letters showing that his name was sent to London in 1819.

There is one lengthy minute of this Chapter in August 1826 when one gentleman and two lawyers were proposed for Exaltation. Two of them being present were admitted. Three of the Companions asked to be admitted to the degrees (sic) of Joshua, Haggai and Zorobabel (sic) and two other Companions requested to be Installed as Masonic Knights Templar the next March. The Chapter then closed in Harmony and Brotherly Love.

In November 1828, there is the last Minute when two more lawyers were Exalted and those members in distress were given assistance. There, the Chapter ended until its resuscitation in 1894. It must have seemed indeed that the Holy Royal Arch was going nowhere.

As we leave matters there, what is to be learnt from the necessary diverse and selective discoveries that I have tried to share with the reader?

If there are those who have access to their own records of this period and believe that what is there could be of interest I would be pleased to see them, and if there is another edition of this work perhaps we can include them there.

Whilst it seems that there is enough evidence of what Bernard Jones described as the *'somewhat chaotic state'* at this time, seen from a Grand Chapter point of view, it can also be affirmed that whilst individual Chapters pursued their own agendas and even perpetuated older customs, Royal Arch Masonry was at least kept alive and well in many parts of England.

When it was given its new shape, clear Provincial leadership and control, it was able to flourish.

Journey's End

It will, I think, be clear from the evidence of the previous chapter that in many parts of the country there was a growing desire to have the same care and attention paid to the Holy Royal Arch ceremonies and organisation as was evident in the Craft.

After all, it was 20 years since that first Union took place and the Duke of Sussex, who had taken such a keen interest in the Craft's welfare and growth, would still be able to direct any necessary changes to this sister 'Order' and introduce the administrative improvements that would support any fresh approach.

Accordingly, in February 1834, just 21 years after his former role as Grand Master began, a Committee under the Duke's chairmanship was set up and included Lord Dundas, John Ramsbottom, and six other distinguished Companions, with, especially, the Revd George Adam Browne.

This latter figure was well-known to the Duke, having served as H.R.H's chaplain for a time and having composed a musical piece for the Duke's birthday celebrations in 1817.

He was a Brother of many attainments, being a Fellow of Trinity College, Cambridge, and having been Grand Chaplain and even First Grand Principal when required.

His tenure of the Grand Superintendency of Cambridge and Suffolk lasted for 22 years. His experience and standing were to be of great importance in launching the 'new look' for what we have seen was an ancient but varied and, latterly, a somewhat neglected Rite.

By early November the committee had a report to submit for the Grand Officers' consideration and, on receiving their general approval, another meeting on 21 November 1834, was arranged for presenting the new forms, not merely of the rite for Exaltation, but for the Installation of the Principals and the especially new feature, the three Lectures to be regularly delivered by their Excellencies. It was at this meeting that the express thanks of the Excellent Companions were given to the Revd Adam Browne *'for his attention to the welfare and interest of the Order.'*

As had happened in the rearranging of the Craft ceremonies, the catechetical lectures, which had recapped on what a candidate had done and learnt during his Exaltation, were wholly dispensed with and whilst the change must have made the occasions much shorter and perhaps more palatable there was a great deal of instruction about, and insight into, the ritual, which was now lost.

I now know, as a much older Mason, what the late and much revered Masonic scholar, Bro Colin Dyer, meant when he said to me, just before he died:

'The worst and most lasting mistake at, and after, the Union was the total removal of the old Lectures.'

It is interesting and informative when attending many North American ceremonies to note those very lectures retained and regularly used.

From February 1835 a special Chapter of Promulgation was warranted for six months to assist in the dissemination and adoption of the new Royal Arch workings. The aim, in this case, was to try and ensure uniformity of working throughout the Order and so serious was their intention that the Grand Principals were prepared to threaten the suspension of any Chapter that did not teach the accepted ritual. As far as the main body of the ceremony is concerned it does appear to have been the case that in the Chapters of the Home Counties the objective was attained though that is not part of the story of this journey. What is still clear from certain of the oldest Chapters in the areas farthest from London is that there was not disagreement but bewilderment as to exactly what was being expected, especially where such Chapters did not, or could not, arrange for one of their number to attend the rehearsals of the new working in the South-east.

As a possible fresh insight into the outcome of this momentous time in English Royal Arch Masonry it so happens that a piece of ritual evidence was recently resurrected in, not the crypt, but the cellar of the oldest extant Masonic meeting house in Bolton, Lancashire.

The ritual in question is a clear, handwritten copy of what someone transcribed after returning from the south in July 1835. Here at least we have an authentic copy of what was the new Royal Arch ritual which was acquired by Bro Matthew Blunt, First Principal of the Chapter of Concord.

He obtained this copy when he was deputed by the Lodge Anchor and Hope No. 37, and subsidised by the Companions and Brethren, to attend Grand Chapter *'who were holding Meetings for Instruction in order that there might be one general mode of working'*. So begins this document.

As has been already intimated the new ritual was of a very much shorter length, without any semblance of an extended Opening, the ceremony of the Veils, or the recitation of the previous catechetical 'lectures'.

However, since we now have a verbatim presentation of what was to be the Holy Royal Arch for the future I propose to run through the text highlighting what are possible variations from the working most familiar to us today. If the Chapters to which any readers belong now use the same form as that here recorded then I hope they will be pleased to know the ultimate source of their practice and appreciate its antiquity.

Those whose workings differ in any substantial fashion may be led to wonder why, in their case, the Duke of Sussex's committee did not have its way.

Interestingly, the text begins by giving the two Latin table graces which we still use and one wonders if this is not a reminiscence of the former days when Masonic business was all conducted around a table at which they both recited and ate.

What I find odd is that though the first grace is given a correct translation as '*May the Blessed One bless (our table)*,' the second grace is, as I believe is still the case today, wrongly translated. It should be '*May it (that which we have partaken) be blessed by the Blessed One.*' Their text gives: '*Blessing and praise be to Him who is the Blessed One.*'

We now turn to the 'Opening of the Chapter' and the Bible is opened at Isaiah chap.12. This is a hymn of thanksgiving that contains the following verses:

> '*The Lord gives me power and strength; he is my saviour...*
> *Let everyone who lives in Zion shout and sing.*
> *Israel's holy God is great and he lives among his people.*'
> It is, I think, significant that the very next chapter begins
> '*This is a message about Babylon...*'

On the pedestal ONE WORD is formed and covered. All the Companions as they enter give the S. and W. to Scribe N. at the door after which the Principals enter robed.

They form a triangle with each Principal repeating the words and they then advance by one step at a time using the 'O' words. The Z. calls for prayer and J. uses the Anglican collect still used by us, but adopting the Supplicatory sign in reverence.

The Principals then approach their chairs, all walking abreast with the Z. moving up the centre of the chapter room, H. on the North and J. on the South. They all pause as Z. unveils the TABLET on the pedestal. They then form a triangle:

'Rt. foot, left hand and right arm upright resting in hollow, knees touching.'

After the word they '*press their chairs with their knees*' as they take their sceptres and repeat the words silently.

J. then replaces the veil that Z. removed.

Z. (Knocks) *Asks the P.S. 'What is the care of every RAM?'*

P.S. *To see the Chapter properly tiled.'*

Z. *Asks* Comp. N. *'see the Chapter properly tiled.' (N. affirms)*

Z. *Asks* Comp. P.S. *'What is our next care?'*

PS. *'To see that none but RAMs are present.'*

Z. *'To order as RAMs. Comp.SN.do you vouch all as RAM?'* (Does)

Z. *'To order as RAMs: let us offer up our prayers to the M.H.'*

J. *'May the glorious Majesty of the Lord our God be upon us, prosper thou the work of our hands upon us. O prosper thou our handiwork. S.M.I.B.'*

Z. declares the Chapter open with four knocks repeated.

During the risings before Closing the MEZ says:

'Is there anything for the good of RAM for the 1st time of asking?' (You can tell an Anglican parson has devised this)

There is nothing specific for the Second Rising but the Third is for RAM in general and the Fourth for this Chapter in particular.

With knocks by Z. alone, and 'all upstanding', Z. asks P.S. about constant care and N. is asked to prove close tiled. The P.S. responds that the next 'constant care' is to appear to Order. The Principals form the triangle as at the opening and then all the Principals kiss the open Bible and Comps. kiss a closed one.

J. is now asked to deliver this prayer; all with the reverential sign:

'Lord of our Fathers and protector of our souls and bodies blessed be thy h(oly) w(ord) for having once more permitted us to call to mind thy wonders of old. If our thoughts have wandered from thee O pardon thou our wandering thoughts and renew a right spirit within us, and may we henceforth flee every wicked desire and shun everything displeasing in thy sight, O God our strength and Redeemer.'

The P.S. is asked to close the Chapter and by command does so. P.Z. says *'Nothing now remains...'* and if time allows there is given the Charge before departure at this point.

The Exaltation ceremony starts with the P.S. going outside to test the Candidate and give him the new P.W., now necessary because the requirement of being a Past Master is no longer required and thus the Past Master's password cannot be used.

The candidate is hoodwinked and with a cord about his waist. The test at the door completed, the candidate is admitted on the F.P.O.F. and put in the West. Among the usual enquiries by Z. the term 'supreme degree' is used.

After a prayer the Candidate is, says Z.,

'to be passed around the Chapter. Companions will take notice that Bro.A.B. is about to pass in view before you to show he is a Candidate properly prepared to be Exalted to this Sublime Chapter'.

There is one circuit of the room and the Candidate is invited to advance *'to the Sacred Shrine'* and *'by each step you approach nearer to the Mysterious Name of the M.H.'*

He arrives at *'the dome of the Vaulted Chamber'* and is *'to draw forth 2 of the Cape stones'.*

Having then figuratively descended, the Candidate, kneeling on the ground hears passages from Proverbs chaps.2 and 3.

The Candidate then searches and *'P.S. puts scroll into his hand'* and all is familiar until he wrenches out the third capestone. Candidate then rises and is told to pull the stone again when he then descends to hear Haggai chapter 2, vv. 1-9 read by H. '*all kneeling*'.

The obligation is as usual but the penalty description is left vacant in this text.

Having sealed the obligation four times the Candidate is raised from the vault and '*restored to the Light of truth*'.

The Candidate sees what we see with Scribes having unveiled the pedestal and then is asked to read from the scroll, after which he is asked to view the pedestal top. Candidate retires.

A report is given and three MMs announced. The pedestal top is veiled. The narrative of the P.S. is as it is today and the Companions take the same implements. On their return the 'Sojourners' describe exactly the same events as today.

The same ritual continues identically to the moment when Scribes E. and N. accompany the P.S. to a certain spot to test his knowledge. The investiture of 'these worthy men' then takes place with the usual wording, and the five Signs are communicated with the following comment:

'*These signs have certain meanings that will be explained fully in subsequent instructions.*'

We have neither these explanations nor any indication of what the new Lectures to be given by the Principals were to be. Neither is there any indication of the Grand Chapters' catechism. The manner of sharing the Sacred Word is then shown to the Candidate and then he is invited to take his place in the Chapter.

This was an obvious, and for many older Royal Arch Companions, a very decisive watershed in the history of the practice.

It is reported that Bro Adam Brown often remarked: '*This is the real Master Mason's degree*' and this Ms copy of the ritual still retained a passage with which my generation were wholly imbued:

'*You may perhaps conceive that you have this day received a fourth degree in Freemasonry but such, strictly speaking, is not the case. It is only the MM degree completed.*'

It must have begun to dawn that a wholly new era was starting. Yet with the extensive, even if not total, severance with its Christian origins, by a discontinuance of the Mosaic exile elements in the Ceremony of the Veils, by the almost total absence of more than the names of the Solomonic Grand Masters and that era of the original tale, and the losing of the close connection of the Royal Arch with the status of a P. Master '*by the waters of Babylon*', a wholly new slant was given to this Order.

What is remarkable is that when presented with sincerity and skill the Holy Royal Arch can still convey something of that special ethos that may help a Craft Mason to realise that he has indeed reached the Summum Bonum; the perfect conclusion, of his essential Masonic journey.

During most of my life it has been my longing that if I was granted enough years to understand and explain the Craft I would then be allowed to expose the earlier years of this Order so as to still appreciate the great tradition behind its more modern face.

That I have now been allowed, thankfully, to do.

We cannot, as with the remains of Fountains or Tintern Abbey, hope to restore the Masters' Past to its original glory.

What we can do is explore its remains with understanding of what once were the reasons for its original shape and function. At least with the Holy Royal Arch we still have a living if emaciated body.

My hope is that by what has been written here there will be many more Masons who will recognise its essential place in our great Masonic family and join it with a clearer picture of what an august heritage they will now enjoy.

Index